A POCKET FULL OF PEACE

RAY R DHARMA

INDIA • SINGAPORE • MALAYSIA

Copyright © Ray R Dharma 2023
All Rights Reserved.

ISBN 979-8-89067-895-9

Contents

A POCKET FULL OF PEACE
The Workbook

My soul cries for enough space,

within which to roam,

but also enough limits,

by which to be guided.

My soul prays for enough silence,

within which to find peace,

but also enough words to express itself.

My soul seeks enough aloneness,

in which to develop,

and enough touching,

by which to announce its presence.

– Anonymous

From the Master's Desk

It gives me immense inner joy to present these insights, my personal experiences in the pursuit of the state of perfect relaxation, nirvana, moksha, enlightenment, call it what you may. I would start off this book by dedicating it to all those who have sought, are seeking and will seek in the future.

Stories of healing have always been close to my heart, maybe it is the repressed fear of death and disease that lurks in all of us or the tribulation in the overcoming of sickness. There is something that touches us when we hear of another human who has, in a sense, defeated the evil disease. This is perhaps why word healing originates from holy. I was counseling adolescents at the time when I first encountered Reiki. We were the first to open a Reiki clinic in Bangalore City; and soon, we saw that we were making quite an impact. Our clients gave us the stature of friend, guide and healer. Reiki was, of course the main element in the healing process there, but I must give an equal share of importance to, firstly, creating a relaxed environment and secondly, to building a friendship rather than a purely professional relationship.

During this period I had several insights into the relationship between the mind and the body. I noticed that although we fear, even hate sickness, there are several dimensions to sickness, a very interesting one being, that it has its payoffs. For example: Ever noticed how a sick person in a house takes centre stage? Everyone around is suddenly converted into a caring slave. We do need the attention some times. But it becomes a trap, because if we are not aware, a pattern sets in, which does not allow any healing to happen. The question that came to mind was - are we at some level wanting things to go wrong so we can find solutions for them? Can we even imagine a life without this constant preoccupation?

When we examine these "problems" do they stem from a 'root' insecurity? And if they do, is there a way to heal at the causal rather than peripheral level... once and for all?

These questions led me to attempt to reach the realm of causality, by unfolding the self, layer by layer, through introspection and progressive self work. What began as a personal search or enquiry, over the years has evolved into this program. The attempt made in this book is to remove myth from natural healing and put forward a logical and scientific understanding of the healing capability of our bodies. 'A Pocket Full of Peace' program contains several methods and techniques I have carefully selected and systematically formulated into a 56 day regime. The aim of the program is to help you get in touch with the calm energy within. The method that will suit you best, is up to you to find, and so is the "getting there". This program can give you a taste of various simple techniques that have been and are being used. When you find the one you know is right for you then you will not require anything else.

Remember however, that relaxation is not a doing, it is a happening and it happens when you begin letting go. There is no way you can force relaxation onto yourself, you'll just be creating more tension. Relaxation is essentially the process of letting go and allowing the natural processes to take over. Hence don't try to relax, just give yourself the permission and let it happen.

May the Universe guide, direct and protect you and shower upon you an abundance of love, knowledge and light.

Kay R Dharma

A POCKET FULL OF PEACE

The Theory

Introduction

A Hole in the Soul

Human behaviour is fundamentally a learnt set of responses to changes that occur within and around us. The scientific knowledge and understanding of these responses may be relatively new; however they themselves are as old as humankind itself and have remained the same over the ages. The brain responds to these changes based on raw data collected by the sense organs that it receives through the nervous system. This, it then interprets and puts into perspective. The body in turn responds to the interpretation by the brain, as it triggers off physical coping mechanisms, through the regulation of hormones - all in a matter of seconds. Every change in the body has a corresponding response by the mind and every change in the mind has a corresponding response in the body. In fact it wouldn't be inappropriate to say that the body and mind are the function of each other.

The human experience lies in the realm of opposites; good and bad, heaven and hell, pleasure and pain. Here we are not questioning which responses are right and which are wrong, rather we ask which ones are healthy and which of them are not. Our context is not one of morality or ethics, but rather one of well-being. During this program we would be exploring two such opposites that although essential to our survival are yet taken for granted; the first is the stress response and the second the relaxation response.

In the beginning, the world was a very dangerous and an unfathomable place. We had to defend ourselves from each other and against powerful enemies not to mention unexplainable natural phenomena. And that too without claws or sharp teeth... our only weapon was our oversized brain and our new found ability to think. Scary times to have lived in.

But we made it through. Then for the first time we could think about other things. The more pain and suffering we encountered the more we fostered the need to seek the meaning and depth to life, to reach a state of understanding, tranquility and bliss. Over the ages formal religion has been the source of comfort for human distress. Religion had been successful in satisfying curiosities to existential questions and had devised ways of experiencing peace with existence. Epictetus, the Greek stoic philosopher said, "there is but one way to tranquility of mind and happiness; let this, therefore, be always ready at hand with thee, both when thou wakest early in the morning, and all the day long, and when thou goest late to sleep, to account no external things thine own, but commit all these to God." Indeed an individual who believes, gains mental comfort and social support to cope with the tragedies of life, but the end of curiosity, more often than not, leads to a self righteous state. This is to say that for another to have a different belief than one's own is evil. The worst part then is that one can see this judgmental quality in others and not in oneself. This phenomenon is perhaps responsible for all wars.

The danger does not lie in having a belief itself; it could be rather beneficial as we can see. The danger lurks in the background as the subject is emotionally charged. For example, if I was to say that I believe that the sky is green, wouldn't make much of a difference to you, as you are not emotionally attached to the color of the sky. But if I was to say my God is better than yours, or that my god is the true god, you would even be willing to kill me to defend your belief. The difference is the emotional attachment.

For a majority of people, religious and spiritual beliefs are a vital part of how they think about their lives, and cope with it. These beliefs can provide:

A sense of meaning and purpose

A framework for setting priorities

A way to place stresses in perspective

Comfort during illness or crisis

Support for a healthy lifestyle

Opportunities for social contact

As our understanding of ourselves and our environment grew, there was need for a structured, verifiable and observable body of knowledge. One that would go beyond emotional bias, one that could unify us as a species, one that would give

> A means of developing supportive relationships
>
> Reasons to help others
>
> A sense of being part of something larger than oneself
>
> A variety of studies find that religious belief and practice is associated with:
>
> - ➤ Less stress
> - ➤ Less risk of self destructive behaviours (suicide, smoking and drug abuse)
> - ➤ Greater overall satisfaction with life.
>
> Pg 39 TIME LIFE MEDICAL'S "The Healthy Mind Healthy Body Handbook" By David S. Sobel, MD and Robert Ornstein, PhD, Patient Education Media, Inc. New York, 1996.

us a better understanding of ourselves and our environment. Hence, science took over the role of answering these questions; it failed however to address the issue of how mankind would deal with this new scientific perception of reality. Science today has gone into so many specializations and sub-specializations, that for one individual to say I know all of science is impossible. Let us also not neglect the fact that religion, although had ways of initiating healthy responses, was not able to incorporate scientific understanding and refused to let go of age old myths and dogma. Hence, asked of its practitioners – to have faith and belief, modern man with his new logical temperament could not easily take to.

The vacuum created thus had to soon be filled, the result -consumerism. It was like mankind broke up the grand relationship, and ended up at the mall. However, this style of living brought with it further complication as these misdirected desires provide only short term relief. Let me explain, first we fantasize about possessing objects, as they are made to seem like the ultimate remedy. Then we go get the fantastic object, only to find that it is not really the ultimate. The truth is that our fascination lies in the unattained. *Once something is attained the glory fades away.* But before we think about this we have already moved on to another object which now seems like the ultimate. And not forget we treat people and relationships like objects as well. Can these achievements truly satisfy? What if you had all the objects you can desire? Aren't they merely substitutes, surrogate fulfillments?

Modern man is left with two choices, to either accept spirituality and to suppress his logical, questioning ability altogether, or satisfy this longing for answers through scientific understanding, and make an appointment with the shrink!

The Road Map

In India, there are said to be four ways of reaching the ultimate - the Bhakti yoga (Path of Devotion), the Gnyana Yoga (Path of Knowledge), the Karma Yoga (Path of Action) and the Dhyana Yoga (Path of Meditation). The term Yoga means the ultimate state of union between one and all that is.

BHAKTI YOGA

To understand Bhakti Yoga, one must let go of understanding. A person on this path relies on emotion. He/she works on becoming sensitive to subtler emotions like devotion, love, compassion, empathy. An experience of oneness with all living things and constant gratitude to the higher powers are part of this path. Prayer and devotional art are the methods adopted in this path to experience peace and tranquility.

GNYANA YOGA

This path entails the refinement of the intellect to such an extent that the individual realizes the truth of existence. This path entails the logical elimination of the illusive and the unreal ego, restraining from one's emotional responses through mind control and the seeking of larger perspectives. It also involves the constant acquiring of deeper level of thought and enquiring into beliefs and patterns that are taken for granted. Tranquility, in this path, is experienced at a state where the individual no longer is concerned with his own pleasures. But sees himself as one with the suffering of the rest of mankind.

KARMA YOGA

The most misunderstood path is perhaps this one. Karma yoga is often understood as the mere performing of certain duties and responsibilities. It is in fact about discarding conditioned patterns of behaviour and moving to a place of spontaneous action. Karma yoga is the dedication to the dynamics of action. So what is action? You might say action is the purposeful movement in a particular direction. Then is it possible to stay actionless? Well, at the macro level we are on a planet that is moving at very, very high speeds around the sun. The sun itself is moving at an even greater speed around the centre of our galaxy. Then the galaxies are moving away from the each other at even greater speeds. At the micro level our bodies are constantly performing activities. Whether you like it or not the brain is constructing new pathways, your lungs are pulling out the oxygen from the air that you have just taken in, your heart is getting oxygen to the rest of the body, and your lunch is being digested and so on. At an even smaller level cells are being born, performing their specified tasks in perfect harmony with their colleagues and being replaced with newer ones constantly. The cells that made you last year, in fact have all been replaced. Action in nature is spontaneous. You might ask if there's anyone *not* on this path? The understanding is that human action is never spontaneous; it is in fact a function of our limited knowledge and experience, and conditioned with the limitations from our past.

DHYANA YOGA

If we were to keep aside all the mysticism and philosophy of religion, what we would be left with is - practices. These include a wide range of techniques that we could broadly classify as-

    a.   Breathing techniques: those associated with manipulation or awareness of breath. Examples of these can be found in the systems of Yoga, Tantra, Tao, etc.

    b.   Physical exercises: those associated with physical movement, posture and workouts. Examples of these can be found in Yoga, Tantra, Tai Chi and the various martial art systems.

    c.   Introspective techniques: those associated with exploring inner realities. These are said to be advanced techniques and are found in different forms in almost all religions.

d. Prayer: those associated with relating with a higher consciousness. Examples of this technique can be found in all religions which have a concept of god.

e. Meditation techniques: those associated with conscious attempt to experience inner peace and tranquility. Widely found in eastern religions.

These techniques although very different from each other, make the common promise of giving relief to the practitioner. They are said to bring about peace, tranquility and balance, and at the same time bring good health to the individual. They also have in common the requirement for a quite place, a comfortable posture and the need for regular practice. The understanding of these techniques of meditation was based on one's personal experience and introspection methods, which the scientist chose to stay away from. This is why in the past, little research was conducted into anything that had a mystical background to it. Fortunately, open-minded scientists have made it possible today for things to be different.

Choosing Health

"The greatest discovery of my generation is that human beings can alter their lives by altering the attitudes of the mind."

– William James (1842-1910), Pioneering American Psychologist

Someday, science may help man eradicate death and disease once and for all, but until then, these are very real issues. The discussion on mortality could go on for ages; here, however let us address the issue of health. So, here's the basic question – should you consider yourself healthy on the basis of there being absence of disease? Or does good health stand for more than what is immediately apparent? Is the meaning and significance of good health different to all of us or is there a common human theme that underlies the occurrence of disharmony? Although, still largely working with the specialized approach to health care, *conventional medical science today has accepted the fact that health is not a mere absence of disease*. In Sanskrit, the ancient Indian language, the word used for health is *swaasth* which is derived from the two word *swa* meaning self and *asthi* meaning established. Here we find the essence of the mind-body approach, which is, that a healthy individual is one who is established, integrated in his self. It is so because only when one understands oneself, does one become aware of the choices one makes. Choices that might be small but could have significant impact on the way one lives and experiences life. According to the United States Centre for Disease Control in Atlanta, Georgia, "Eighty-three percent of deaths for adults between the age of 21 and 65 are related to lifestyle."* The good news, however is that *you* are in charge. *For when you becomes aware of choice, you realize that you hold the power to choose differently.*

____

* "Stress Management for the Health of it" Clemson Extension, Clemson University, HE Leaflet 66, Rep. February 1997

The Information Age

As individuals are becoming more and more aware of lifestyle choices, we find that they are more open and willing to try out several Complementary and Alternative therapies or mind/body approaches. Although a general term, it covers all health care systems, practices and products that are not currently part of conventional medicine. Some therapies that were considered part of complementary and alternative medicine until recently, have now been accepted into conventional medicine. If a therapy is to be used alone it is called *alternative* and if is to be used alongside conventional health care it is referred to as *complementary*. The methods prescribed in 'A Pocket Full of Peace' Program fall under the complementary therapy category, as simultaneous conventional diagnosis, therapy and monitoring is advised.

Even though such medicine have been the main source of health care for large number of people in less-developed countries, conventional medicine in its formative years considered most of it 'mumbo-jumbo'. The coming of the 'information-age' has brought in some new trends. In 2002, a nationwide government survey in the U.S. revealed that 36 percent of adults aged 18 years and over, use some form of complementary and alternative medicine.[*] One of the important factors that have influenced this trend is the growing body of scientific literature from clinical trials. Although quite a few of these techniques have been used over centuries, they lacked scientific validation. Nowadays, however, several such trials are being conducted in the U.S. and all over the world. Other factors include the greater awareness of other

---

[*] "Complementory and Alternative Medicine Use Among Adults: United States 2002", Barnes P, Powell- Griner E, McFann K, Nahin R. CDC Advance Data Report 343, May 27, 2004

countries, cultures and traditions, the need for accelerated healing and also to an extent the sense of being in control.

Over the years, we have been led to believe that for every ailment there must be a specific and unique remedy, prescribed by a specialist in that field. There is nothing wrong with this, however, complementary therapies are usually holistic in nature and treat the person as a whole i.e. body-mind-spirit. Here, as we address root issues, the therapy is aimed at encouraging self-healing by empowering the person. Holistic therapies are hence, often used on a host of ailments. The methods and practices that are part of the 'A Pocket Full of Peace' program utilize this holistic approach.

Note: Also see List of Websites on Page

Relaxation Rediscovered

We experience our life in the following conditions, that is the mind is either relaxed or tense, combined with either high energy levels or low energy levels. The combinations possible are the following four-

'WAYS OF BEING' TABLE

	State of Mind	Energy levels
1.	Tense	High
2.	Relaxed	Low
3.	Tense	Low
4.	Relaxed	High

Out of the four we are generally living in the first three ways of being. Owing to the reason why often relaxation is associated with lethargy and stress and sometimes mistaken for drive. However, as seen in the table the fourth, seems to be the healthiest and easiest way. It is not that we don't experience this state at all, we do, yet it is momentary and we do not possess the techniques for repeating it for ourselves.

Relaxation therapy is a rather new western concept, though in eastern cultures, relaxation is much more than a therapy; it is suggested as a means to self-realization. Most spiritual systems include some methods or techniques for relaxing the mind and attach significance to the experience of tranquility, of bliss, etc. In ancient India, relaxation had a very crucial role to play in growth and development. In Sanskrit the word *shanti* is used to represent relaxation, peace, tranquility and transcendental bliss.

The Hatha Yoga Pradipika, one of the authoritative books on yoga, says, "When the Prana (life-force) becomes tensionless and the mind becomes absorbed, then their (the practitioner/s) becoming equal (balanced) is called Samadhi. When the body becomes lean, the face glows with delight, Anahata-nada (un-heard or un-struck sound, inner silence) manifests, and eyes are clear, the body is healthy, bindu (libido) under control, and appetite increases, then one should know that the nadis (meridians) are purified and success in Hatha Yoga is approaching."

Hatha Yoga Pradipika, The Yoga Shastra Vol XV Part III, Published by Sudhindranatah Vasu, Printed by Apurnva Krishna Bose at The Indian Press 1915

"Mans ancestors with the most highly developed fight-or-flight reactions had an increased chance of surviving long enough to reproduce. Natural selection favored the continuation of the response. As progeny of ancestors who developed the response over millions of years, modern man almost certainly still possesses it."

PAGE 55

Herbert Benson, MD THE RELAXATION RESPONSE, 1975 Harper Collins Publishers

The underlying aim of most Indian *yogic* and *tantric* methods was to attain a state of deep relaxation or *Samadhi*. Reaching and remaining in that state was said to be the ultimate challenge; and the benefits were profound.

One of the earliest mentions in medical science came from Herbert Benson MD, when he coined the term 'Relaxation Response' in the 1970's, to describe a state of the body that is the opposite of stress. To understand relaxation in the scientific manner, the understanding of stress is essential. Walter B Cannon, a physiologist from Harvard, was the first to describe the flight or fight response as a series of biochemical reactions that prepares the individual to deal with danger. Stress is the mind and body's response to anything that is perceived as overwhelming or adverse. The origin of stress is from the time when primitive humans at every step encountered various life threatening situations and required a quick boost in energy to fight or flee from stronger, faster, and more agile predators.

As a self-preservative response, the 'fight or flight' mechanisms are

> "When a single situation requiring behavioural adjustment occurs again and again, the fight-or flight response is immediately activated. Ultimately this repetition may lead to higher blood pressure on a permanent basis. It is our underlying theory that this is what happens in man in the development of hypertension. The chronic arousal of the fight-or flight response goes from just transient elevation in blood pressure to permanent high blood pressure."
>
> PAGE 95
>
> Herbert Benson, MD THE RELAXATION RESPONSE, 1975 Harper Collins Publishers

triggered off and the body and mind undergo certain changes, using up energy resources. This response is natural as it protects the individual, by creating a tense awareness required to avert the danger. This same primitive response has been retained, however triggered off by non life-threatening situations through perceived danger. The stress response most of the time is inappropriate and only leads to aggravation and embarrassment. Today, the stress response could be a trigger by the boss, the colleague, the spouse, a traffic jam, examinations, interviews, criticism, deadlines, competition, public speaking, inflation, financial issues, health issues, children's problems, the list is almost endless.

When You Are Under Stress

Anything one can perceive, one can perceive as a threat. However, as it lies between the stimulus and response, your perception, plays a crucial role. In our lives, when we associate certain specific triggers (things, people, events, circumstances, thoughts or feeling) with stress, we exercise the following options. We either try to desensitize or numb those areas, even to the extent losing touch with the issue, by repressing it, or otherwise, we try to avoid these triggers altogether. It seems to be the logical thing to do yet, this does not cause the stress to reduce in any way rather it gets displaced and transferred to another object. Hence, it forms a pattern, a cycle. This is so because, the external stimulus is merely a trigger, and it is the individual's perception of the stimulus and the body's own stress response, which are the cause of concern.

Hans Selye, the first major researcher on stress was able to trace exactly what happens in our body during the fight or flight response. He found that any problem, imagined or real, can cause the cerebral cortex (the thinking part of your brain) to send an alarm to the hypothalamus (the main switch for the stress response, located in the mid brain). When one is under stress, several physical, mental and emotional changes occur. Not only does this process sap one's energy but over a period of time can lead to a host of disorders at the physical, mental and behavioural levels.

"Almost every system in your body can be damaged by stress. Suppression of the reproductive system can cause amenorrhea (cessation of menstruation) and failure to ovulate in women, impotency in men and loss of libido in both. Stress triggered changes in the lungs increase the symptoms of asthma, bronchitis and other respiratory conditions. Loss of insulin during the stress response may be a factor in the onset of adult diabetes. Stress suspends tissue repair and remodeling which in turn causes decalcification of the bones, osteoporosis, and susceptibility to fractures. Inhibition of immune and inflammatory systems makes you more susceptible to colds and flu and can exacerbate some diseases such as cancer and AIDS (Acquired Immunodeficiency Syndrome). In addition, a prolonged stress response can worsen conditions such as arthritis, chronic pain, and diabetes. There is also some evidence that continued release and depletion of norepinephrine during a state of chronic stress can also contribute to depression."

Pg 3. The Relaxation and Stress Reduction Workbook, Martha Davis PhD, Elizabeth Robbins Eshelman MSW, Mathew McKay PhD New Harbinger Publications, 1996

At the **physical level** under stress, the body's defense mechanisms are initiated, adrenaline is pumped into the blood stream, the heart pumps faster; leading to stress induced hypertension, blood pressure rises, and in some cases palpitation experienced. Breathing becomes faster and less efficient leading to breathlessness and even hyperventilation. Dilation of pupils, muscle tension increases and could lead to headaches, dizziness and even insomnia. Sexual desire is suppressed and may lead to loss of libido, impotence, interruption of menstruation; and digestive processes slow down leading to digestive problems and ulceration. The immune system is also suppressed increasing the risk of disease. Other effects include sweating, blushing, clamming hands and feet, etc, with the experience of physical fatigue afterwards. Chronic stress may lead to high cholesterol levels, high blood pressure, gastrointestinal disease and weakening of the immune system.

At the **mental level,** 'tense-energy' is experienced. Thoughts may become jumbled or confused. Another indicator is that thinking becomes focused on worry. It becomes much harder to concentrate, make clear judgments or find solutions. This usually leads to low productivity and inability to meet deadlines, further aggravation and eventually mental fatigue. Over a period of time excessive stress can influence thinking, learning and recalling ability.

At the **emotional level** people respond to stress in many different ways. Common emotional indicators are irritability, impatience, anger, frustration, fear, anxiety, self-doubt, panic, despondency, feelings of inadequacy, insecurity, emotional withdrawal and depression.

At the **social or behavioural level**, there are indictors like becoming isolated, less caring, more hostile and insensitive. Short-temperedness, volatility and irritability are also changes that might occur. Many people respond to stress with excessive eating, drinking and smoking.

How Bad is it?

Stress pervades all aspects of our modern life. From the hurry of the breakfast table, to the wading through traffic and reaching our destination.

The following is an excerpt from the BBC News Health report, titled '**Most workers stressed**', dated Tuesday, 30 January, 2001.

More than four out of five workers believe the work place has become more stressful over the last five years, a survey has found. More than two-thirds of those who took part in the survey said they felt either stressed or under pressure at work. And nearly three-quarters (73%) said their performance was affected by stress.

The research was carried out by the income protection insurance company- *Unum*. The results are based on the responses of more than 1,200 workers in full and part-time employment. Workplace stress expert Professor Cary Cooper, of the University of Manchester Institute of Science and Technology (UMIST), said: "Until now, employers have associated stress with the occasional headache or day off work. However, they should be really concerned when three-quarters of workers say their performance is affected by stress."

Unum's own figures show that the number of mental and psychological claims have risen by 88% over the past seven years. Those for chronic fatigue syndrome are up by 40%. Professor Cooper said: "The Unum survey confirms that a combination of long working hours and an autocratic management style are key sources of stress in the workplace. Employers need to move away from long working days as this does not result in increased efficiency - only increased levels of illness. Managers should become more oriented towards a greater praise and reward culture, and should also adopt more flexible working arrangements to help strike a better balance between home and work."

The Other Side of the Coin

> "We are what we think.
>
> All that we are, arises with our thoughts.
>
> With our thoughts, we make our world."
>
> Gautama Buddha

All the above being the effects of stress on the individual on various levels, relaxation has the opposite effects. That is, a decrease in metabolism, blood pressure, oxygen consumption and heart rate, leading to accelerated healing counteracting the negative effects of chronic stress.

When the individual is relaxed he/she experiences calm energy as opposed to the tense energy experienced during stress. And just as stress leaves the individual tired and exhausted, relaxation leaves the individual rejuvenated and recharged. When made part of the daily routine, it helps reverse the aging processes and also bring about transformations on the mental and emotional level, which then lead to accelerated growth and development of the practitioner.

"Our studies revealed that the opposite was also true. The body is also imbued with what I termed the Relaxation Response- an inducible, physiologic state of quietude...Regular elicitation of the Relaxation Response can prevent and compensate for, the damage incurred by frequent nervous reactions that pulse through our hearts and bodies."

PAGE 9 (revised Foreword, 2000)

Herbert Benson, MD THE RELAXATION RESPONSE, 1975 Harper Collins Publishers

Based on this theory, several relaxation techniques have been tried and tested over centuries and new ones keep evolving, as per the need of the times. Most involve repetition and focused awareness (of a word, sound, phrase, breath, body

"Unlike the fight-or-flight response, which repeatedly brought forth as a response to our difficult everyday life situations and is elicited without conscious effort, the relaxation response can be evoked only if time is set aside and conscious effort is made.

Our society has given very little attention to the importance of relaxation. Perhaps our work ethics, views a person who takes time off as unproductive or lazy. At the same time our society has eliminated many of the traditional methods of evoking the Relaxation Response. Prayer and meditation as practiced by the ancients have become part of our ancient historical memory. We need the Relaxation Response even more today because our world is changing at an ever increasing pace."

PAGE 185

Herbert Benson, MD THE RELAXATION RESPONSE, 1975 Harper Collins Publishers

sensation or muscular activity), others use guided imagery, passive muscle relaxation or some form of meditative exercise. They are generally grouped into Long-term or Deep methods (autogenic, meditation, progressive muscle relaxation, etc.) and Short-term or Brief methods (self controlled relaxation, paced respiration, deep breathing, etc.), these generally require less time to acquire and practice, other methods could include Hypnotic techniques, Biofeedback techniques and Cognitive Behavior Therapy (CBT).

Further, science has ventured into the study of the mind-body connection and has begun to acknowledge the natural healing and rejuvenating capabilities of the mind and body. Techniques which help create the appropriate conditions for the acceleration of these rejuvenation processes are thus gaining credibility. The mind and body have the capability of replenishment and renewal. When people ask me is relaxation therapy tough? I tell them it couldn't be simpler, in just four words 'relax and let glow!' All that really needs to be done as far as relaxation therapy is concerned is to find the methods that are best suited to you and with them achieve a relaxed state. Just being in that state will not only take care of accumulated stress but will help create an inner stability that will help deal with whatever lies ahead. As the Swiss psychologist Carl

Jung (1875-1961) said, "The word happy would lose its meaning if it were not balanced by sadness. It is far better to take things as they come along with patience and equanimity."And when one begins the experience of inner equanimity and harmony, there is not only an immediate transformation in one's attitude but has also positive repercussions for the people around.

Scientific Evidence

And in 1999, the federal government, based in part on testimony I gave before the US House of Representatives and the US Senate in 1998, appropriated $10 million to the National Institutes of Health to create Centers for Mind/ Body Interactions and Health across the country. The Centers will conduct mind/body research and training. The Senate Fiscal Year 1999 Appropriations report states:

... The Committee recognizes that stress contributes to a host of medical conditions confronted by health care practitioners, and current pharmaceutical and surgical approaches cannot adequately treat stress related illnesses. Mind/Body approaches, particularly those of the relaxation response and those related to utilizing the beliefs of the patients; have been used successfully to treat these disorders. The Committee is aware that the Harvard Medical School is at the forefront of research on mind/body interactions and their clinical applications. The Committee is encouraged by the results

Researchers have studied relaxation therapy for the treatment of following health problems by means of clinical trials. Research shows possible effectiveness for anxiety, depression, pain, insomnia, premenstrual syndrome and headaches. However, as relaxation therapy as a science is in its infancy, further well designed research is needed to confirm these results and make strong recommendations.

➤ **Well-being**

Studies using relaxation to improve well-being in multiple types of patients show positive results. Increased levels of calm, with a resultant improvement in psychological well-being, have been demonstrated.

➤ **Stress**

Relaxation with audio and group training sessions has shown decreased stress in study participants.

of this research and the health and cost benefits of mind/body approaches. The Committee encourages OBSSR [Office of Behavioral and Social Sciences Research] to establish pilot mind/body medical centers to make more visible the benefits of mind/body medicine; to expand its scientific base; and teach and train health care professionals in these approaches..."

PAGE 36-38 (revised Foreword, 2000)

Herbert Benson, MD THE RELAXATION RESPONSE, 1975 Harper Collins publishers

"How wonderful it was in the1990s to have peers begin to traverse the chasm, to swing from the ropes over the artificial divide between mind and body that we are systematically taught. In 1992, an endowed Harvard professorship was established in honor of our work. This professorship will be named after me upon my retirement. Wonderfully, courses about mind/body medicine and spirituality are now an established part of the curricula in most medical schools everywhere, and are some of the most sought-after classes among aspiring physicians.

In 1995, we achieved another scientific milestone. The National Institutes of Health, the worlds leading source

➢ **Anxiety**

Numerous studies in humans suggest that relaxation therapy may moderately reduce anxiety, phobias such as agoraphobia (fear of crowds), dental fear, panic disorder and anxiety resulting from severe illnesses or before medical procedures.

➢ **Depression**

Early studies in humans report that relaxation may temporarily reduce symptoms of depression.

➢ **Insomnia**

Several studies suggest that relaxation therapy may help people with insomnia fall asleep and stay asleep longer. Cognitive (mind) forms of relaxation such as meditation may be more effective than somatic (body) forms such as progressive muscle relaxation.

➢ **Smoking cessation**

Early research reports that relaxation with imagery may reduce relapse rates in people who successfully completed stop-smoking programs.

➢ **Headache**

Preliminary evidence suggests that relaxation therapy may help

of medical research funds, devoted a "Technology Assessment Conference"- a prestigious assemblage of experts- to assess relaxation and behavioural approaches. They concluded that relaxation techniques should be incorporated into the treatment of all forms of chronic pain.

(Contd.)

reduce the severity of headaches in children and migraine symptoms in adults. Positive changes in self-perceived pain frequency, pain intensity and duration, quality of life, health status, pain related disability and depression have been reported.

➢ **Premenstrual syndrome**

There is early evidence that progressive muscle relaxation may improve physical and emotional symptoms associated with premenstrual syndrome.

➢ **Menopausal symptoms**

There is promising early evidence from trials in humans supporting the use of relaxation therapy to temporarily reduce menopausal symptoms.

➢ **Asthma**

Preliminary studies of relaxation techniques in humans with asthma show a significant decrease in asthma symptoms, anxiety and depression, along with increases in quality of life and a significant improvement in measures of lung function.

➢ **Irritable bowel disease**

Early research in humans shows that relaxation may aid in symptom prevention and relief of irritable bowel disease.

➢ **HIV/AIDS**

Mental health and quality-of-life improvements have been seen in preliminary studies of HIV/AIDS patients.

➢ **Tinnitus (ringing in the ears)**

Relaxation therapy has shown positive results in studies of tinnitus patients.

➤ **Angina**

In preliminary research, relaxation was shown to reduce anxiety, depression, frequency of angina episodes, medication need and decreased physical limitations.

Note: Also see List of Recent Studies on Page

Relaxation...

☑ **Rejuvenates the body and mind**

Research also shows that meditative techniques increases the levels of melatonin, an important hormone produced by the pineal gland that supports the immune system and promotes deep and restful sleep; slows cell damage and aging; improves energy levels and may even inhibit the growth of cancer cells.

Traditionally, relaxation has been the means to an end, the end being spiritual in nature; a deep meditative state. However, as we have seen it could also help with various physical, mental, emotional and behavioural diseases and disorders. Just as the stress state brings about a cascade of negative changes, the relaxed state brings about a cascade of positive changes.

☑ **Accelerates natural healing processes**

Complementary relaxation therapies can also be used during treatment for chronic pain, burns, wounds, post operative recovery, diabetes, gastritis, gastrointestinal disorders, heart disease and repetitive stress injuries, since relaxation stimulates the immune system and brings about significant rejuvenation, in turn also reversing the process of aging and improving longevity. It also can help with insomnia, mental fatigue, fears and phobias.

☑ **Improves self-image**

It has also been noticed that individuals who are usually in a calm energetic state, establish new levels of self reliance, worthiness, self esteem, confidence and self comfort. With the new found calm energy, meeting deadlines, sales targets, making presentations, handling angry customers, all becomes rather effortless. Hence, also facilitates in achieving one's desired goals.

☑ Brings clarity of thought

With relaxation a sense of peace, tranquility and well being is experienced and as a result facilitating resolving of issues like fears, anger, road rage, and panic disorder among others. Relaxation can also bring to life, latent creative abilities, thereby, equipping you with adaptability: which is responding creatively to change beyond conditioned responses.

☑ Improves concentration and memory

The calm energy state improves focus and enhances multitasking abilities. It also helps improve retention and academic performance in children and students alike.

☑ Facilitates sexual intimacy

Firstly, sexual energy is suppressed when the individual is under stress and often what also comes in the way of sexual intimacy is worry about issues relating to family or the workplace. There are also underlying conflicts, guilt, fear associated with intimacy. Relaxation helps in overcoming these obstacles and can help enliven the relationship.

☑ Helps transform undesired behaviour patterns

Relaxation therapy can facilitate in overcoming addictions, alcohol abuse, and social phobias.

Note: Although relaxation therapies are considered safe for healthy adults, they are not recommended as the sole treatment for potentially severe medical conditions. Under no circumstance should they delay or come in the way of diagnosis and treatment from a qualified health provider. Please read the disclaimer carefully before attempting any of the prescribed techniques.

PROGRAM GUIDE

Program Content

A Pocket Full of Peace program brings to you the collective benefits of some of the most effective and advanced relaxation therapies, like Guided Visualizations, Reiki, Music therapy etc. The guided visualizations will get you set to take on the day and help cleanse accumulated stress and rejuvenate after work so you have more energy to spend on other activities. Reiki and Music therapy work at a sublime level, brings you closer to a natural state of blissful relaxation.

Why A Pocket Full of Peace program?

- ☑ It consists of a few minutes of self-work that facilitates dealing with stress at the causal level and gives birth to a whole new outlook to life.
- ☑ You do not require any previous knowledge, belief or experience to begin the program.
- ☑ The techniques can be easily learnt and practiced in the convenience of your own home.
- ☑ It has been designed to fit into the busiest of schedules.
- ☑ You could customize the program to apply greater emphasis on what you identify as a problem area.
- ☑ The workbook is designed to give you the feeling of participation in the work. Contains background, step by step explanation and benefits of techniques, making it very comprehensive.

Program Format

> "Knowing is not enough; we must apply.
>
> Willing is not enough; we must do."
>
> -Johann von Goethe

A Pocket Full of Peace program has been divided into three phases, and are as follows:-

Phase I: Preparation

The first phase, 'Preparation', is about getting warmed up with some small additions to your daily routine and creating a readiness; physically, mentally and emotionally, for what lies ahead. Apart from the morning and evening practice, it includes three basic techniques.

Phase II: Transformation

This phase, 'Transformation' is about tapping into one's inner healing capacity to create a healthy self, beginning with a healthy self-image. In this phase is the important chakra work-out plan.

Phase III: Harmonization

And finally, phase three 'Harmonization' entails practical application of the new personal experience and achieving a stress-free inner state of calm energy during all activities. In this phase, you will learn to use your re-discovered abilities in the various aspects of your life.

Workbook Layout

This "power-packed" workbook contains a description of the selected techniques, its explanation backed with a complete step-by-step procedure. The workbook prescribes the easy, systematic and efficient way of getting the maximum benefits from activities given in (a) workbook and (b) the audio file. For easy access and comprehension, it is presented in the following layout.

Background:

Includes a short introduction to the technique, acknowledging its origins and enlisting some of the reported benefits.

[Note: there may be several other benefits that have not yet been reported, the ones given in the workbook are only those which practitioners have experienced.]

Technique:

Step by step instructions of the method with a brief description of every step.

Notes:

Includes special instructions and other relevant information, as and when required.

Work space:

The work space is meant for the practitioner to make personal notes of issues, experiences, comments, etc. after every exercise. You could have subliminal experiences and discover your potential, during the program. It is

"Once you have made the decision, the universe conspires to make it happen."

Ralph Waldo Emerson

recommended that you make note of all such occurrences, understandings and insights. These notes form a very good source for future reference. It is also recommended that your notes be kept personal and private.

Steps to Initiate the Program

STEP 1: the possibility

Compassion for myself is the most powerful healer of them all.

- Theodore Isaac Rubin, M.D.

Watching your thoughts is the starting point. As you do this, you will begin to notice patterns. The program works on the fundamental assumption that a transformation is possible at this level. During the program, it is normal to find yourself slipping back into old patterns; however, you must be able to maintain your focus on the possibility of transformation, and treat any obstacles as the learning required to reach your destination. This has to be step one, and since you have chosen a program for self-work, you have already taken the first step. The process has already begun, now all you need to do is drop any reluctance, resistance or lethargy that you feel right now and take the plunge. Think of it as a bungee jump, as long as your thinking about it, you're not doing it; and if you're doing it, you wouldn't be thinking!

STEP 2: the time and space

The next step is *you*; your time and your space. The program although flexible, requires a certain degree of consistency and commitment. The best way to do it is to set a time and some personal space for the practice. Tell yourself that this is my time and I deserve it. By doing this, you would create a routine that soon becomes part of your life and also give the green signal to your natural healing processes to take over. The simple task of creating a neat clean space for these personal practices will also act as a signal of your openness to positive change.

STEP 3: the intention

> "Anything less than a conscious commitment to the important is an unconscious commitment to the unimportant."
>
> - Stephen Covey, Ph.D., First Things First

The next step is the intention, the *declaration* that you will make it work for yourself. In other words, give yourself the permission to "relax and let glow!" The program also requires a certain degree of honesty and integrity. More than the details, it is the intention that is the driving force of the program. The guide describes the program over 56 days which is a 'fast-track' module, however, you know yourself best. So in case you miss an exercise, be sure to go back to it rather than trying to finish the program in a hurry. If you feel you need to repeat any part of the program, feel free to do so. At the end of the program you would find that a few practices have comfortably and almost effortlessly become part of your routine.

STEP 4: the support structures

At this stage, it is important to view some issues that might seem to come in the way of your practice. Again the emphasis is on self-awareness, as you know what is best suited for you.

➤ Professional guidance: Before you begin with A Pocket Full of Peace program, please read the disclaimer carefully and seek professional advice and if required a general physical checkup as well.

➤ Illness: Sound physical and mental health is the basic requirement for the practice of this program. If you are suffering from any serious or chronic ailments, it is advised that you get the professional help that you require, before starting the practice of the exercises in this program. Please contact us for any clarification in this regard, we would be happy to be of any assistance to you.

➤ Thoughts: If during practice you are disturbed by unwanted random thoughts, let them arise without any efforts to suppress them. Watch them with complete detachment, like a witness, and continue the practice. In the beginning, when there is a lot of accumulated stress the frequency of thoughts could be high. Gradually, you would find that as your stress baggage

If you're looking to turn back the clock on your body, Shanti Johnson, an associate professor of nutrition, advises eating a broadly based diet that packs a nutritional punch:

1. Dark green leafy vegetables such as spinach (calcium, iron, folate and beta-carotene)
2. Sweet potatoes (folate, beta-carotene, vitamins A and C, and fibre)
3. Blueberries and other dark berries (vitamin C, iron and fibre0
4. Yogurt (calcium, protein and phosphorus)
5. Beans (iron and a high fibre form of protein)
6. Whole grains (higher in fibre than white bread, with more B vitamins, vitamin E, selenium and zinc)
7. Nuts (according to a recent American stud eating them more than five times a week could cut death rates from heart disease by 25 to 39 percent)
8. Salmon, tuna and other cold water fish (omega-3 fatty acids)

"Want to live to be 100?" Camilla Cornell, Readers Digest Vol. 163 August 2003.

diminishes, so will their frequency. It will then become easy and fluid for you to focus your awareness. This quality of witnessing the mind and its thoughts is the first step into meditation.

➤ Languaging: *"Pleasant words are a honeycomb sweet to the soul and healing to the bones"*, a phrase from the Bible (Proverbs 16:24). When we use the word *'affirmation'* we'd usually imagine it to mean, a string of flowery words used to intensify positive thinking. But the important truth is that, anything put into words is an affirmation. Every mental thought has its physical counterpart. Hence, e-v-e-r-y-t-h-i-n-g we say or think about is an affirmation. This is to say that in our practice of relaxation as a regime, we must learn to become more and more aware of our words, and of our languaging.

➤ Strain: Do not strain yourself physically or mentally under any circumstance. Regular daily practice will gradually bring flexibility and positive changes to the body and mind, which in due course would make your practice easy and effortless. Make sure to wear loose flowing and comfortable clothes during practice. Be aware of your breathing through the exercises; do not hold your breath for any longer than that is comfortable.

- ➤ Methods: To get the best out of the program, (a) make sure *you have understood each step* before you begin, and (b) during the practice of the techniques keep a check on *following all steps correctly.*
- ➤ Diet: Food is the first source of life energy. Your diet can also help prevent illness and disease. Make sure you get four balanced meals a day.

It is also recommended that you undertake a detoxifying diet program under the supervision of a qualified nutritionist. You could do this either before or during the program.

- ➤ Water: The recommended intake for adults is 8-10 glasses of water a day. Water helps transport vital nutrients; regulates body temperature; eases digestion; keeps joints supple; cleanses out our body; keeps skin healthy and young. Not drinking enough leads to dehydration, resulting in headaches, fatigue, dizziness, constipation, and foggy memory. Water plays a major role in supporting liver function.
- ➤ Breaks: *"Every now and then, go away, have a little relaxation, for when you come back to your work your judgment will be surer. Go some distance away because then the work appears smaller and more of it can be taken in at a glance and a lack of harmony and proportion is more readily seen"*, said Leonardo Da Vinci, the creative genius. A small *mental vacation* during work can recharge you, and in turn increase and enhance your productivity.
- ➤ Humour: *"If a man insisted always on being serious, and never allowed himself a bit of fun and relaxation, he would go mad or become unstable without knowing it"*, said the Greek philosopher Herodotus. It is as relevant in the modern scenario. Make humour a part of your day. *To torture the cliché, 'laughter is the best medicine.'*

THE WORKBOOK

Phase I: Purification

"The most beautiful and most profound emotion we can experience is the sensation of the mystical. It is the source of all true science. He to whom the emotion is a stranger, who can no longer wonder and stand rapt in awe, is as good as dead. To know what is impenetrable to us really exists, manifesting itself as the highest wisdom and the most radiant beauty which our dull faculties can comprehend only in their primitive forms, this knowledge, this feeling is the center of true experience."

- Albert Einstein

The theme of this phase is to get in touch with the way we experience our life. The preparation is about, firstly, understanding ones physical needs; secondly, creating an empowering daily routine of self-work; and thirdly, learning to focus the -usually scattered- awareness. This phase will form the basis of the foundation to the program and provide the required preparedness for the next phase, which would be the core of the program. The duration of this phase is 21 days.

Basic Daily Routine

Background:

The QR Code to the audio is a compilation of guided visualizations and musical tracks based on Indian classical music. The purpose is to form a fundamental daily routine which then becomes the base for the rest of the program.

GUIDED VISUALIZATIONS

In the 1970's, Carl Simonton developed a visualization technique that helped individuals with cancer and other tumors, to contribute to their own healing. Since then, many other self-healing visualization techniques have

been developed. Visualizations have been practiced under the guidance of experts to reduce and control pain, lower blood pressure, cure phobias and even turn average athletes into good ones. The two visualizations have been selected to provide specific benefits in the areas of relaxation and rejuvenation, keeping in mind the lifestyles, stresses and needs of the modern individual. The audio set includes two dynamic visualizations, the Liquid Gold visualization and the Unconditional Love visualization.

TRACK 01: INTRODUCTION AND PRAYER

TRACK 02: RAY'S UNCONDITIONAL LOVE

The body-mind connection

Ray has adapted and evolved this technique from the Autogenic 'Self-regulation' Relaxation technique, developed by Dr. Johannes H. Shultz and Dr. Wolfgang Luthe of Germany, which has more than 50 years of medical documentation to prove its effectiveness.

Autogenic training is based upon passive concentration and body awareness of specific sensations. Since the last century, it has been successfully applied in relieving most stress-related disorders. The affected person learns to use the techniques in relieving stress symptoms such as anxiety, tension, sleep disorder, and examination stress as well as in chronic stress induced medical conditions.

Ray leads you through her Unconditional Love technique, where you systematically move your attention and awareness from one body part to the next, using verbal cues to regulate breathing and bringing about warmth and relaxation. It thus enables you get in touch with your body and its needs. It is a positive and life affirming way to beat everyday tensions and stresses. Progressive relaxation of your muscles reduces pulse rate and blood pressure as well as decreasing perspiration and respiration rates. Deep muscle relaxation when mastered can be used as an anti-anxiety pill.

Practicing this meditation at the end of the day would give you immediate and tangible results of relaxation and rejuvenation. Over a period of time its practice will promote overall good health and well-being.

MUSIC THERAPY

In the author William Shakespeare's words, *"When griping grief the heart doth wound, and doleful dumps the mind oppresses, then music, with her silver sound, with speedy help doth lend redress."* Music is known to appeal to our inner being so powerfully that it can enhance and accelerate the natural rejuvenation process of the mind-body. This therapy employs sound in an organized and rhythmic form to disentangle the stressed out nerves, relaxing the mind-body as a whole. Certain sounds have telling effect upon the state of our brain. Most of the sounds heard in the world today are 'discharging' sounds, draining the brain of its vital energy. Sound therapy is a method of beneficially recharging the cortex of the brain and distributing the latent energy throughout the nervous system.

Also, as the music appreciation center is located in the right hemisphere of the brain, while listening to music, one 'switches-over' from the left hemisphere (dominant for binary activities) to the creative right hemisphere. Surveys on the effect of music therapy reveal that favorable musical vibrations can promote a positive thought process in an individual.

Modern therapeutic science says that music has a massaging effect on our brain. Perhaps, that is the primary reason for widespread usage of music as anti-anxiety and antidepressant therapy, thus making it the handiest tool for relaxation. A study found that stress induced increase in subjective anxiety, heart rate, and systolic blood pressure, were prevented by exposure to music, and this effect was independent of gender.*

So, each day massaging your brain with a few moments of soulful tunes and melodies could be a great way to getting positively charged.

In every culture, music arose from devotional chants and invocations. In India, schools such as yoga and tantra equate Nada Brahman, the primordial sound, with the Absolute. The origins of Indian music can be traced back to the chanting of the Sama Veda nearly 4,000 years ago.

*Relaxing music prevents stress induced anxiety, systolic blood pressure and heart rate in healthy males and females."- Knight WE, Richard PhD NS. Monash University, Victoria, Austrailia. J Music Ther. 2001 Winter, 38(4): 254-72

Technically, Indian classical music is said to have two basic elements, the *Raaga* (may be roughly equated with the western term mode or scale) and the *Taala* (the rhythmic form). Raagas are songs in specific notes, forming an integral part of Indian Classical music; they are believed to have their own characteristics, moods and identity.

The hypnotic effect and the direct communication of this music seem to be remarkably effective in calming the troubled mind. Despite the various studies and experimentation, the scientific understanding of the benefits of Indian Classical music is still in its infancy. There are several subtle benefits yet to be discovered and documented.

The two instrumental music tracks have been composed and arranged by Sujit-Rajesh based on Indian classical raagas. The raagas selected for this compilation are *Raaga Mishra Shivaranjini* and *Raaga Hamsadhwani*, due to the healing and relaxation they immediately bring. We have added a modern flavor to make it easy listening, yet at the same time have not diverted from the essential notes.

TRACK 03: RAY'S LIQUID GOLD

The golden fluid protection

This visualization was created by Ray. In her own voice, she leads you through this visualization and helps you create a protective shield around yourself. This shield then acts as a filter and keeps out any stress triggering stimuli and at the same time checks the stress response.

This meditation is best practiced in the morning as you start your day. Within a few days you will notice that you are not only avoiding the negative but more importantly are attracting more and more positive people and circumstances. Over a period of time, it helps in transforming your perspective in such a way that you begin to see only the positive even in the negative.

TRACK 04: Mystic Forest

This soothing composition is based on the *Raaga Hamsadhwani*.

TRACK 05: Om Namoh Narayana

This enchanting composition is based on the *Raaga Mishra Shivaranjini*.

Technique:

We begin the program with including three basic practices into the daily routine.

MORNING: As soon as you wake up,

Step 1 Drink a glass of lukewarm water with just a few drops of lime.

Step 2 With closed eyes, listen to track 4 – **'Mystic Forest'.**

Step 3 Follow this with the visualization **'Liquid Gold'**.

Step 4 And conclude the morning activity with Morning affirmations.

MID DAY: On returning home, after work before you do anything else, freshen up, change into your home attire, and,

Step 1 With eyes closed, listen to the **'Om Namoh Narayana'** Track.

Step 2 Follow with the **'Unconditional Love'** visualization.

NIGHT: Just before you hit the bed,

Step 1 Listen to **'Om Namoh Narayana'** followed by Bed time affirmations.

Note: Apart from the music on the audio file, you could access and utilize the natural sounds all around you. Nature has a vast repertoire of soothing and rhythmic sounds. We seem to overlook the sounds of ocean, breeze, rustling of leaves, bubbling sounds of a cascade and even the sound of silence (anahata nad or the *un-struck sound* in yoga). Listen to the note they transmit, then go deeper into the sounds and listen to the note behind them. Then let the sounds resonate through your entire body, washing away the tensions and worries.

Make sure that during these 56 days you get at least 100 hrs of music therapy.

Breathe Easy Technique

Background:

When it comes to relaxation techniques, I would recommend you try out as many as possible in the beginning. Learn the traditional methods from genuine teachers, which in this case could be the traditional Pranayama technique from your local yoga instructor. The 'breath' in Sanskrit is referred to as *prana*, which is also the word used for 'life', and the two are synonymous. If you were to monitor your breathing patterns, you would notice that they are synchronized with thought and emotion patterns. When the mind is relaxed, so is the breathing and vice versa. This technique is a short and handy one. It involves awareness of breath and has been known to provide the following benefits,

- ➢ Gain immediate relaxation
- ➢ Dissolve excess tension in the body and mind
- ➢ Calm the mind

Technique:

Step 1 Begin this exercise, sitting comfortably, with eyes closed.

Step 2 Take in three nice-long-slow-deep breaths into your belly, holding for a few seconds before breathing out. Although exercise begins with three controlled breaths, is more about breath awareness than breath control.

Step 3 Repeat the following affirmation silently to yourself. (Three times)

"This is my time. This is my space.

Here I can be relaxed.

There is nothing I want, right now.

There is nothing to be done, right now.

There is nothing to be said, right now.

There is no problem to be solved, right now.

Life will flow on, with or without me.

I am relaxed, right now."

Step 4 For the next three to five minutes, breathing normally, allow your awareness to flow with the breath, gently in and out. If you are more of a visual person, you could imagine white light flowing in and out. Or, you could listen in to the soft hissing sound that the breath makes in the process.

Step 5 Take a few moments to remain silent and enjoy the relaxed state you're in. Then gently begin massaging your eyes with your fingertips and slowly open your eyes. You could move and stretch your hands and legs slowly and regain awareness of the world around you, while retaining the tranquility within.

Simple Yogic Exercise

Background:

This exercise routine is adapted from the ancient Indian Surya Namaskar (The Sun Salutation) Technique, which is practiced at dawn facing the rising sun. The following exercise routine is a combination of twenty four positions which are performed in a cyclic rotation (i.e. the first and last positions are the same). It works on (warms up and stretches) all major muscles.

Note: This is a simple exercise that can be practiced anywhere and anytime, especially, when you catch yourself getting angry, anxious or tense. It can be done at home, at your work place, at a traffic jam (not if you are driving), wherever you find the time and space appropriate for keeping your eyes closed for a few minutes. With practice you will find that you can reach a deep relaxed state almost immediately.

Technique:

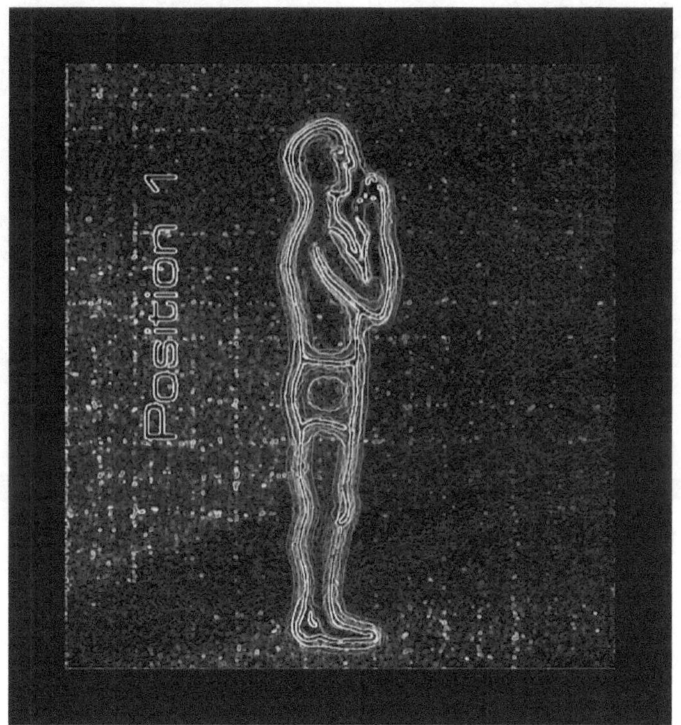

POSITION 1

Stand erect with feet together.

Place the palms together in front of the chest.

Relax the whole body starting with the shoulders.

Breathe normally.

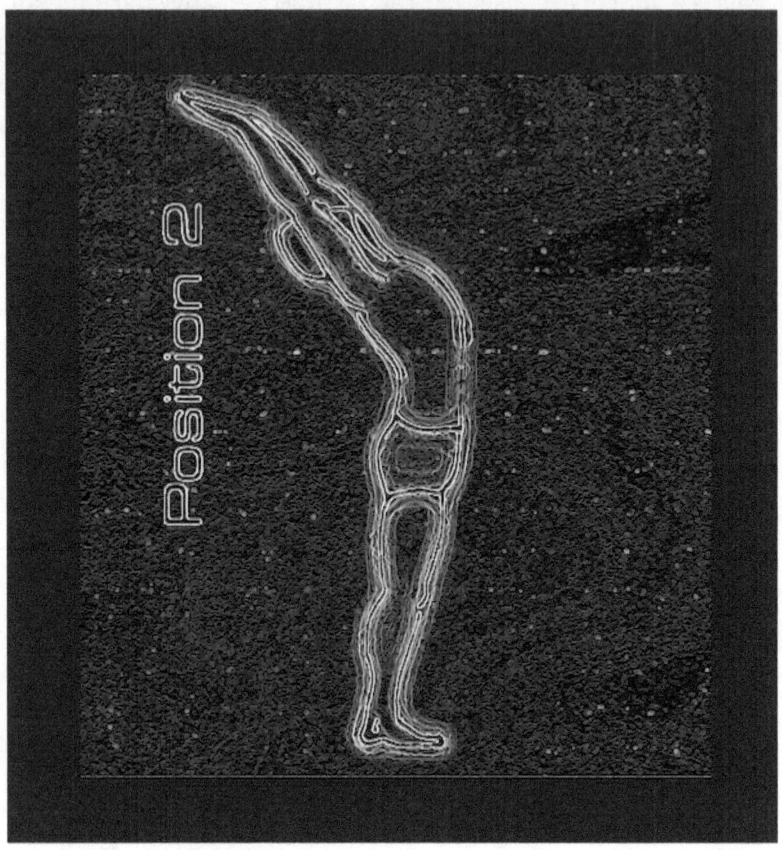

POSITION 2

Raise both arms above the head.

Keep arms apart at shoulder width.

Bend the head and upper body slightly backwards – stretch.

Inhale while raising arms.

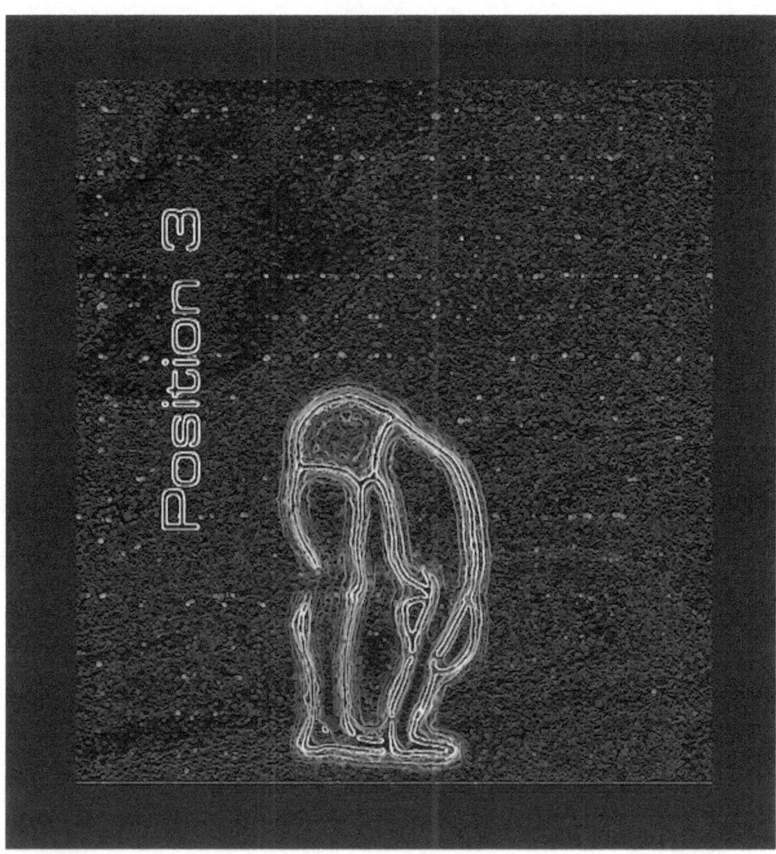

POSITION 3

Bend forward until the fingers touch the ground, either by the sides or in front of the feet.

Keep legs straight.

Exhale as you bend forward.

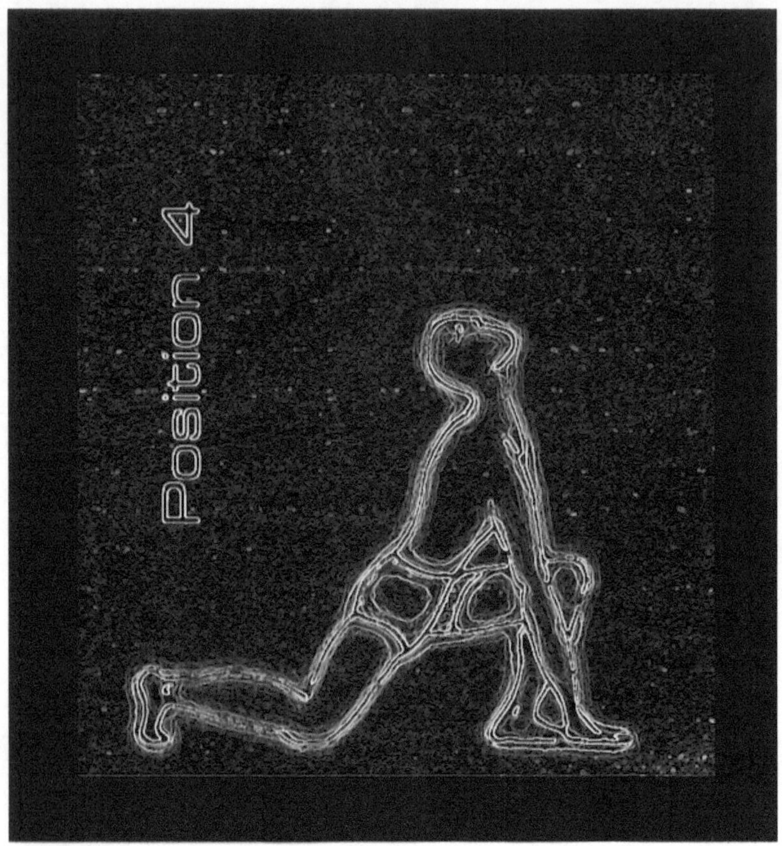

POSITION 4

Stretch the right leg back as far as possible.

At the same time bend the left leg, but keep the left foot in the same position.

The arms remain straight in the same position.

At the end of the movement the weight of the body should be supported by the hands, the left foot, the right knee and the toes of the right foot.

In the final position, the head should be tilted backwards, the back arched and the gaze directly upward.

Inhale as you stretch the right leg backward.

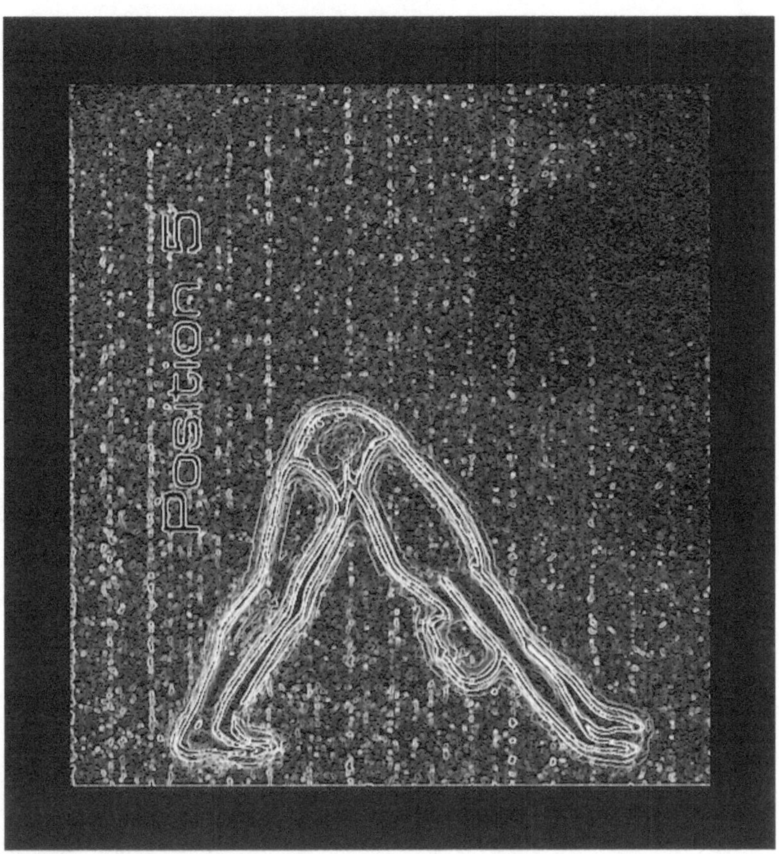

POSITION 5

Stretch the left leg backward and place the left foot along with the right foot. Raise the buttocks and lower the head between the two arms. With legs and arms straight and heels in contact with the floor, the body should form two sides of a triangle.

Breathe out as you straighten the left leg and bend the upper body.

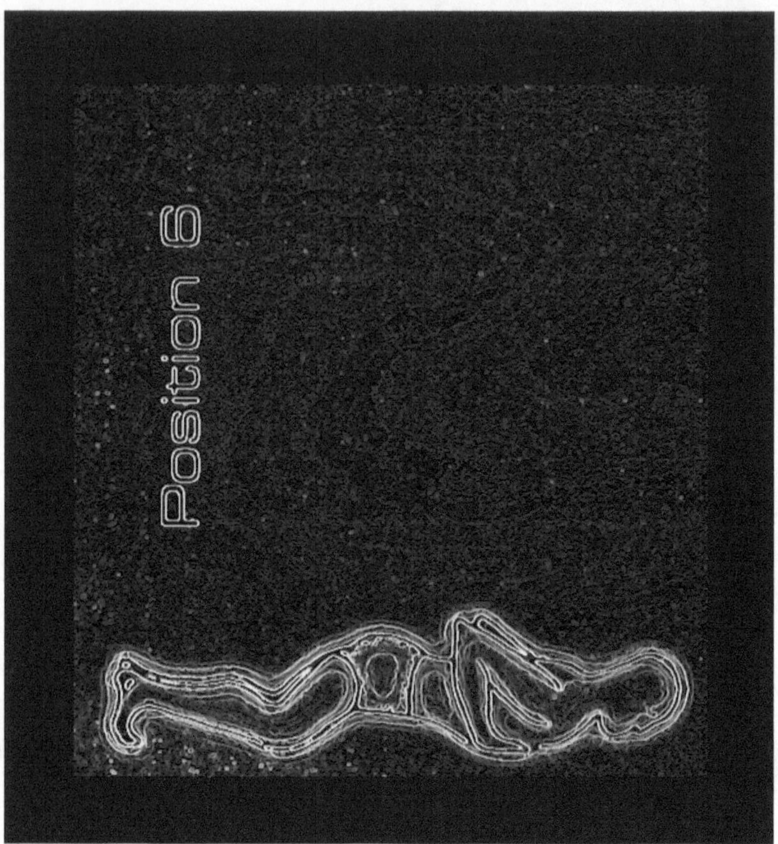

POSITION 6

Lower the body to the ground, so that in the final position only the toes of both feet, the knees, the chest, the palms and the chin are in contact with the floor.

The hips and abdomen should be raised slightly off the ground.

Ideally, the breath is held outside during this posture.

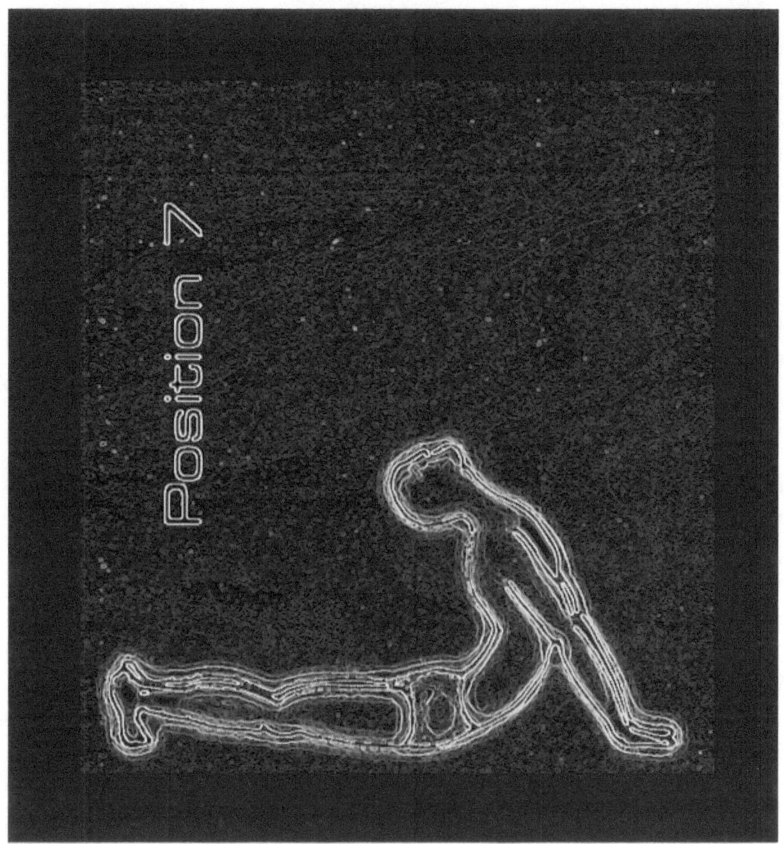

POSITION 7

Raise the body from waist by stretching the arms.

Bend the head backwards.

Inhale as you raise the body, arching the back.

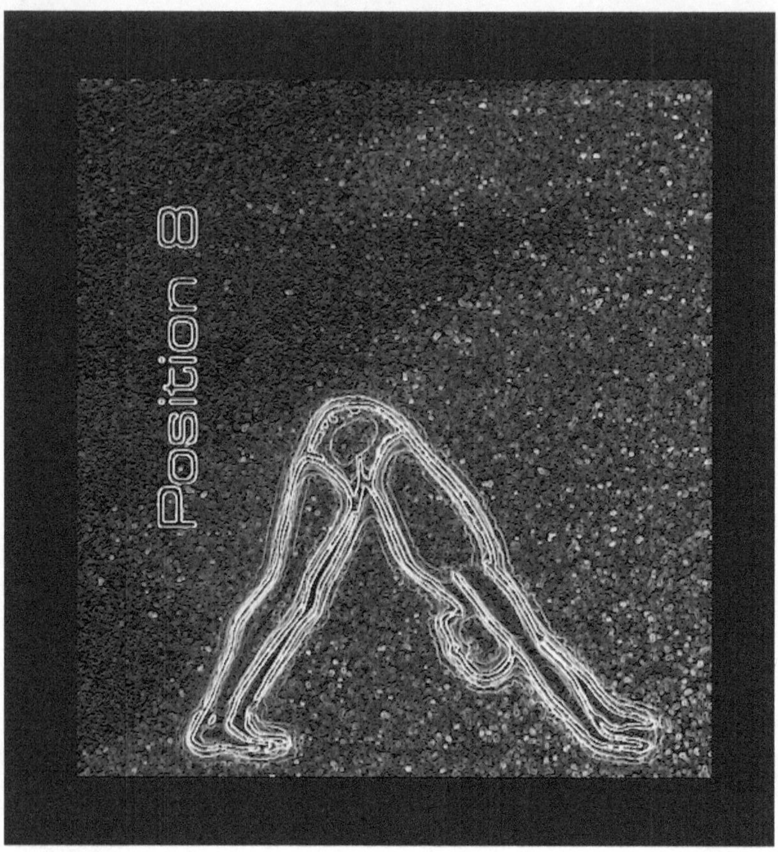

POSITION 8

From the arched position, assume the triangular pose as was described in position 5.

Exhale as you raise the hips.

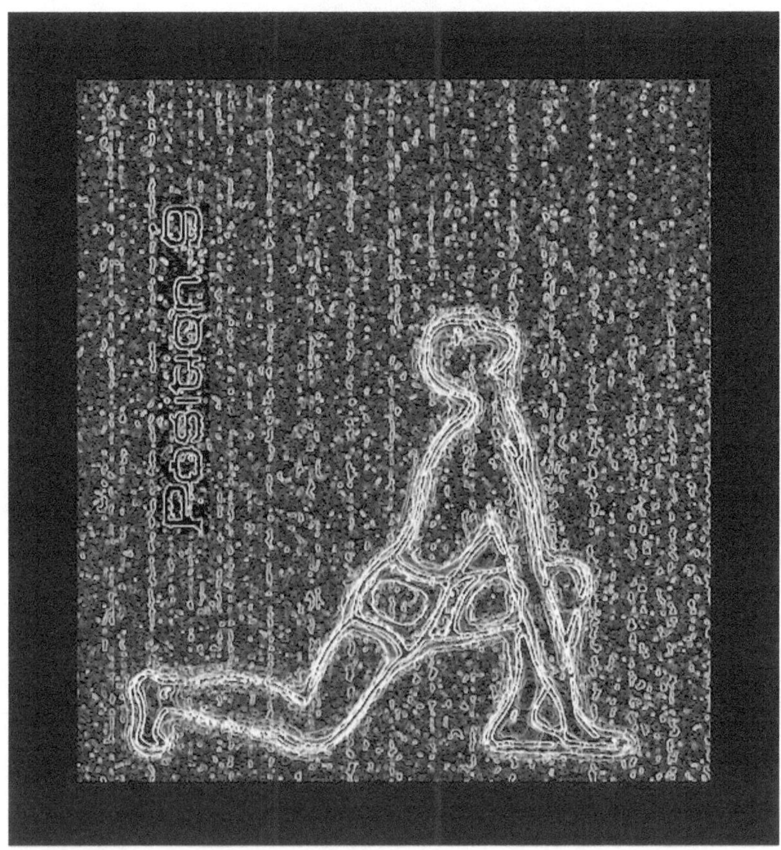

POSITION 9

Same as position 4, bend the left leg and bring the left foot forward.

Simultaneously lower the right knee to the floor.

Inhale as you assume this position.

Note: One complete round consists of 24 postures. We have shown here 12 positions, with the right leg brought forward and the left leg stretched back in the lunging positions (position 4 and 9). The same twelve are to be repeated but with the opposite leg lunging forward and the right leg extended back. Thus, one completed round would have twelve positions with the right leg forward and then twelve with the left leg forward.

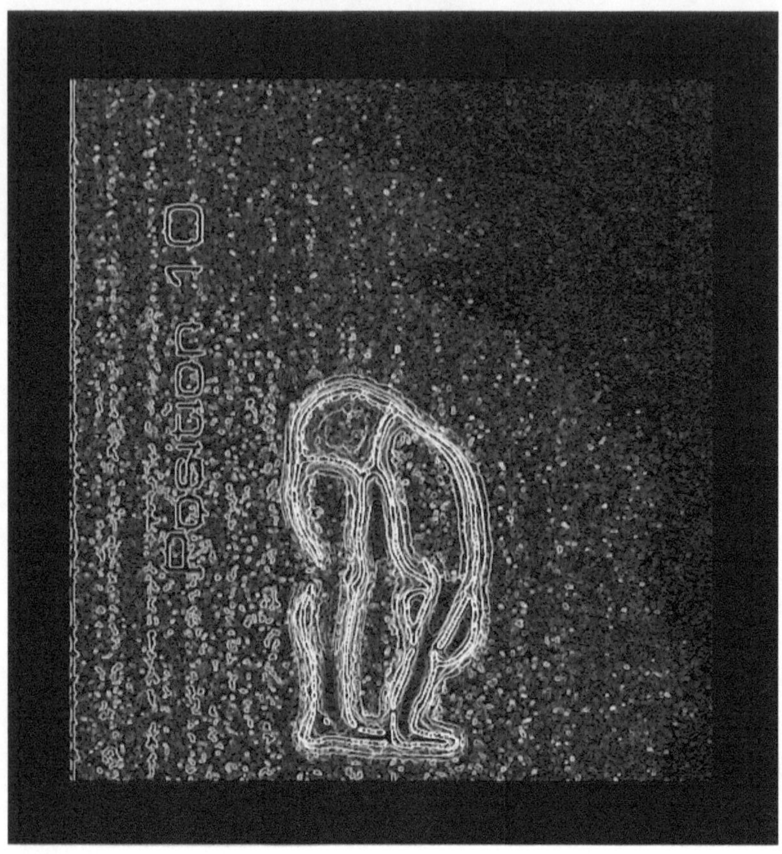

POSITION 10

Same as position 3.

Place the right foot next to the left foot.

Straighten both the legs and try to bring the forehead as close to the knees as possible. Do not strain.

Exhale while performing the movement.

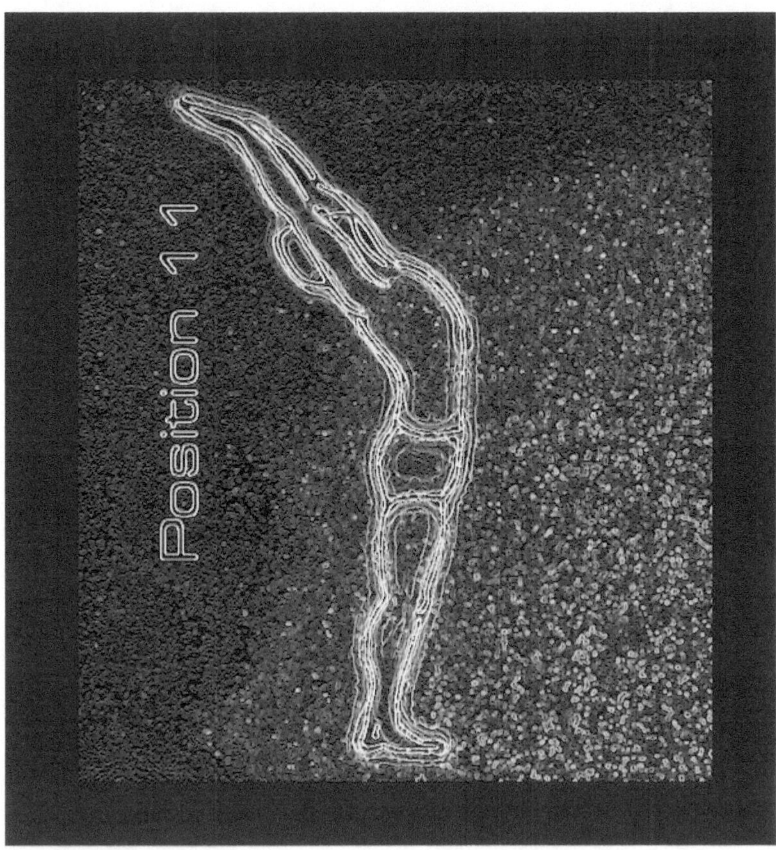

POSITION 11

Same as position 2 straighten the whole body and raise arms above the head.

Bend head and arms slightly backward.

Inhale as you straighten the body.

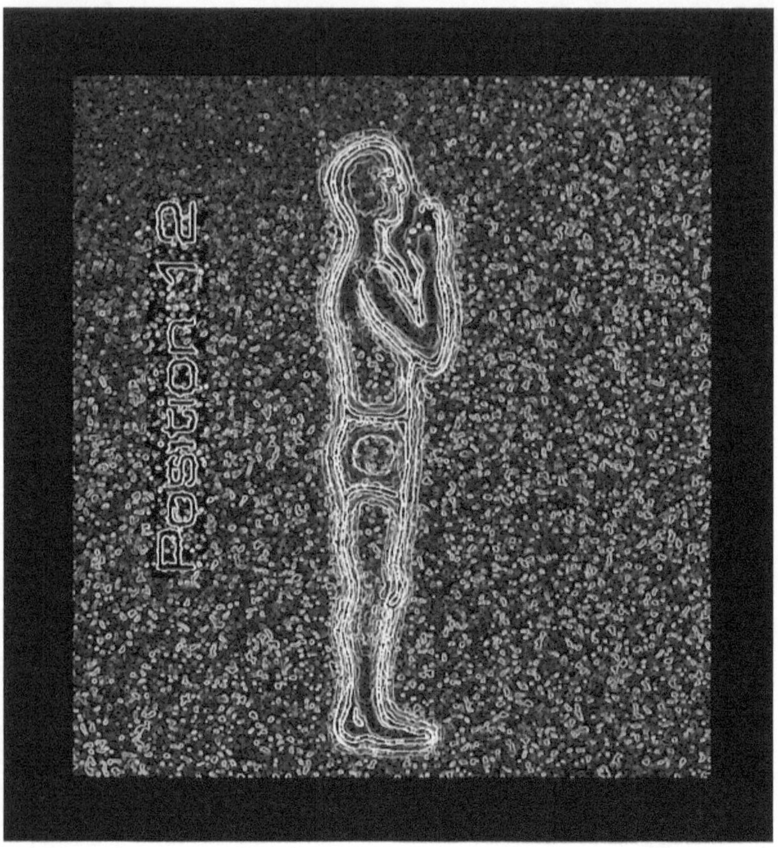

POSITION 12

Same as position 1.

Exhale as you assume this position.

Note: If at any stage of this practice you experience any doubts, discomforts or difficulties, stop practice and seek expert guidance.

If you are suffering from backaches, spinal problems or knee problems, do not attempt this exercise 1) before consulting your physician and 2) without expert supervision.

Focused Visual Awareness Technique (Fvat)

Background:

This exercise has been designed based on the yogic technique called *'Triatak'*. It is a simple yet effective way to bring your consciousness to a single pointed awareness. Practicing of this technique can also help in the practice of more advanced techniques.

Technique:

Step 1 Hold the FVAT sheet at arm's length and at eye-level, and then close your eyes.

Step 2 Take three nice-long-slow-deep breaths into your belly, and then slowly open your eyes.

Step 3 Maintain a steady gaze at the black dot. Allow your consciousness to flow towards it getting concentrated like the sunlight through a magnifying glass. Do not blink during this time.

Step 4 When your eyes feel tired close them. With your eyes closed you could visualize a negative (in this case a white) dot. When the dot fades away, you could begin another round.

FOCUSED VISUAL AWARENESS TECHNIQUE SHEET

Note: You could begin with three rounds a day and slowly go up to about 12 rounds a day. Once you feel you have become comfortable with the technique, you could go on to the next stage in which you will not need the FVAT sheet. But instead focus on the point between the eyebrows, with eyes closed.

Phase II: Transformation

"The softest thing in the universe overcomes the hardest thing in the universe. That without substance can enter where there is no room. Hence I know the value of non-action. Teaching without words and work without doing are understood by very few."

- Lao Tzu, Tao Te Ching 43

- Albert Einstein

This phase is about throwing the light of awareness into the various aspects of your life. This light would get you in touch with areas that you have unconsciously avoided. The cathartic transformation process is not about consciously solving problems, but rather about, giving the subconscious the right signals so it can transform itself.

In this phase, we continue with the basic practices, breathing technique and physical exercises, further adding on the following exercise.

The 33 Day Chakra Workout

Background:

Most people are familiar to the eastern chakra system thanks to martial arts and alternative therapies. For those who haven't encountered it, a simple definition would be, that chakras (literally meaning centre, wheel or cycle), are esoteric energy centers that regulate the inflow of fresh life force and the outflow of used life force, to and from an organism. The human being is said to have seven chakras, the location of these have been discovered to be in relation with the endocrine system of the body. *"As portals between the physical and spiritual planes, chakras represent the sacred architecture of your body and psyche."**

Each chakra is said to not only perform physical functions but also regulate the personality, and are associated with specific mental states, emotions and spiritual growth. Every chakra has its unique color, sound and deity.

Special Note: Kundalini Rising- Awakening the chakras

The concept of Kundalini has been defined in several ways since ancient times, it is however a personal experience. It exists in a dormant state and is said to be situated at the root of the spine. It is the energy that lies dormant within us all and thus awakening of the Kundalini has been said to be the purpose of meditative practice, and the purpose of the human incarnation.

As you work with chakras, you will find their hidden power getting awakened. The process entails moving from the lowest (root) chakra to the highest (Third eye) chakra. The seventh chakra Sahasrara or the thousand petal lotus is never described, as it is said that on the awakening of the sixth chakra or the third-eye chakra, the way to the final chakra is automatically revealed to the aspirant.

There are several books available today for a deeper understanding of the subject. It is recommended that practice of awakening the Kundalini must be initiated and supervised by an authentic Guru or Master.

*Anodea Judith, Ph.D., Chakras wheels of life, 2004

The chakra workout exercise given here however, is a safe and simple way to begin ones personal journey towards transformation. Practitioners have found that one of the many benefits of this exercise is that they began to notice pointers and signs as to how spiritual practice would evolve.

It is made up of two parts, i.e., the workout plan and the silver lining technique. It is spread over 33 days and could be repeated as many times as you may find necessary. It has a logical sequence and is easy to remember, though you could record the steps in your own voice and play it back, since you are required to keep your eyes closed during the practice.

Technique:

The daily method of practice is given below. You would be working on the various chakras based on the specific chakra of the day, as is given in the day-wise chakra workout plan.

Step 1 Begin by sitting in a comfortable position and closing your eyes.

Step 2 Start off with the Breathe Easy technique and focus your attention on your breath for a few minutes. Build your focused awareness point as practiced in the FVAT.

Step 3 Move your focused awareness point onto the location of the chakra on the spinal chord. For some people it may be easier to focus on the location on the front surface of the body. You will be able to intuitively find the location, it is said to be magnetic in the sense, that your attention or focus would be attracted to its centre.

Step 4 Once your attention has rested on the specific chakra, begin this stage of the exercise by gently and normally breathing into the centre. This stage is further divided into three levels, i.e. the physical, the mental and the metaphysical. (The idea is to bring your focus on to the various functions of the chakras and to the various issues pertaining to them. Move from one to the next, visualizing and feeling each issue as relevant to your personal life.)

At the **physical level** begin with visualizing the various internal biological processes, intending that they are functioning smoothly. You could repeat, silently, the following affirmation,

> I declare that my ______ chakra is efficiently performing all its physical functions.

However a recurring headache for example may not be the ailment in itself. It could be caused due to various other factors like hunger, eyestrain, lack of sleep, etc. Hence, as we begin the healing of the physical symptom, we can expect the real issues to come to the surface, to get our attention. Generally, it is suggested that we move with the flow and follow our instincts. If we are dealing with a specific physical symptom, very often we can achieve results simply by directly addressing the symptom. This is simple, easy and can relieve symptoms quickly. For this, silently repeat the following affirmation three times-

> "I acknowledge my ________________ (e.g. headache, indigestion, etc), as my bodies way of communicating to me. I accept my responsibility of taking care of my physical form. And give myself permission to be free of this ____________ and begin my healing."

While most of these issues can be addressed with Relaxation Therapy, it should **not** be assumed that one can relieve symptoms with relaxation and thus permit the ongoing abuse of the body.

At the **mental level**, is an exercise called 'the first time'. In it, you explore each emotion and issue to great depth, with an attempt to reach the first event in your life that you felt that particular emotion or dealt with that specific issue. Some of these events could still have a very distressing emotional effect on you, hence it is suggested that before you commence this part you repeat this affirmation,

> "I am calm and effective in dealing with my issues, at the causal level and do not experience any unpleasant emotions and memories associated with it."

If you're not able to recall specific incidents at first, don't give up. Move to the next issue and you could get back to it at a later time. Eventually, you will be able to recall it, as at the subconscious level our mind stores each and every event of our lives. Please note however that this exercise is not about problem solving. (We are not consciously dealing with the issue here; rather we get to the root of the emotion.) Use this stage to find out what stresses you and why. You could make a list of these for reference during practice.

The next stage would be to ask the question, "If there was an emotional contributor to this physical symptom, what might it be?" Sometimes you may feel that you may not know, in which case you could take a guess. You will be surprised at how often the guesses are accurate. Some examples could be,

- A deep feeling of lack and low self-image, caused by one's unfulfilled wishes and unrealistic self expectation.
- A feeling of inadequacy caused due to the pressure of matching up to the expectations of one's parents or society. This could be big, since one is often unaware of it.
- A deep fear that was established in childhood and is carried over to the adult belief system.
- An emotional issue that has been pushed under the carpet due to the belief that nothing can be done about it.
- A deep set guilt for something left undone or unsaid.

Dealing with these hidden issues is often uncomfortable and requires patience and creative approaches. But once they are dealt with at the causal level, one experiences **new freedom**.

At the **metaphysical level**, visualize the chakra rotating and operating at its optimum. If you are unable to visualize declare it so. Also ask for guidance from the chakra with regard to any disharmony or issues that might have come up. Finally express your gratitude to the chakra for the role it plays in your life.

Step 5 After a minute or two of silence slowly, begin to open your eyes.

THE 33 DAY CHAKRA WORKOUT PLAN

The following is the day-wise chakra workout plan. The technique described above, is used by adding, the specifications of each chakra given in the work out plan. Several additional details have been included to support your visualization. The technique also forms the starting point of the journey to the causal level of the relevant issues. Although the Mooladhara is said to be the first chakra, we ideally could begin this exercise with the third eye chakra ~ the chakra for intuition and knowing. Starting with the third eye chakra would help us in getting a better understanding of the rest of the chakras and their respective characteristics and functions.

Note: During the day be aware of your thoughts, keeping in mind the issues you are dealing with. You would have a constant reminder if you wear some clothing or accessory of the color of the chakra you are working on. You might find that the stress they had regarding a given event or person has turned into sadness. These different emotional aspects would take you closer to the causal level. So watch out for opportunities to make breakthroughs in areas you find yourself restrained. They are opportunities for greater healing for all kinds of stressors. They present to you with great possibilities for mastering the art of relaxation. Also watch for cues and pointers towards the most beneficial course of action, as you get in touch with the power of your inner intelligence.

(See the chakra charts to know the specific colors of every chakra.)

ILLUSTRATION: Location of the Chakras on the human body

Day 1, 2, 3, 4, 5, 11, 18 and 25

Third Eye Chakra

Chakra Name	Third Eye Chakra
Sanskrit Name, Meaning	Ajna Chakra. The word *ajna* in Sanskrit means to know or to command. It is the centre of latent transcendental energy.
Location	Between the eye brows
Color and Element	Indigo and transcendental
Sense	Dhyana or Meditation
Endocrine System	Pituitary and pineal
Body System	Nervous System (both central and autonomic)
Physical Organs	Brain
Emotions and Issues	Higher emotions like creativity, intuition, ESP and issues related to spiritual growth.
Affirmation for the day	Key words: Transformation, Transcendence, Ascension "I am in touch with my inner Guru (Master), and manifest his form and grace in everything around me."

DAY 6, 13 and 20

Root Chakra

Chakra Name	Root Chakra
Sanskrit Name, Meaning	Mooladhara Chakra. *Mooladhara* in Sanskrit comes from the words *moola* meaning root and *adhara* meaning source. It is the centre of survival energy.
Location	At the tip of the spinal chord (Sacrum)
Color and Element	Red and Prithvi (Earth)
Sense	Smell
Endocrine System	Adrenals
Body System	Excretory System
Physical Organs	Kidneys, bladder
Emotions and Issues	Safety, security and fulfillment of basic needs, confidence and time and money related issues.
Affirmation for the day	Key words: Abundance and grounding "I am in touch with my inner reality, and allow it to keep me firmly grounded in reality at all times."

DAY 7, 14, 21

Hara Chakra

Chakra Name	Hara Chakra
Sanskrit Name, Meaning	Swadhisthana Chakra. *Swadhisthana* in Sanskrit comes from two words, *swa* meaning one own and *adhisthana* means dwelling place or residence.
Location	There is a contradiction in various modalities as to the location of this chakra. But as it is intuitively found is it safe to assume for now that it is around the navel or slightly below it. It is the centre of sexual energy.
Color	Orange and Jal (Water) Element
Sense	Taste
Endocrine System	Gonads
Body System	Reproductive
Physical Organs	Sex Organs
Emotions and Issues	Desire, drive and sensual pleasure, issues related with sexuality, self image and life goals.
Affirmation for the day	Key words: Pleasure and Fulfillment "I am in touch with my sexuality, I am peaceful, content and fulfilled with what is and isn't."

DAY 8, 15 and 22

Solar Plexus Chakra

Chakra Name	Solar Plexus Chakra
Sanskrit Name, Meaning	Manipura Chakra. *Manipura* in Sanskrit comes from the words *mani* meaning jewel and *pura* meaning city. It is the centre for power and control energy.
Location	Soft spot in the middle of the rib cage at the diaphragm.
Color and Element	Yellow and Agni (fire) element
Sense	Sight
Endocrine System	Pancreas
Body System	Digestive
Physical Organs	Liver, Stomach, Intestines, Appendix
Emotions and Issues	Authority, power, mental and emotional tenacity, wisdom, Issues related to need for control.
Affirmation for the day	Key words: Control and Power "I am in touch with my power and wisdom, and allow it to humbly guide me towards the letting go of my need to manipulate people and events."

Day 9, 16 and 23

Heart Chakra

Chakra Name	Heart Chakra
Sanskrit Name, Meaning	Anahata Chakra. Anahata in Sanskrit means the un-struck or unheard. It is the centre for love energy.
Location	Middle of the chest
Color	Green and Vayu (air) element
Sense	Touch
Endocrine System	Thymus
Body System	Circulatory and Respiratory
Physical Organs	Heart and Lungs
Emotions and Issues	Love, hate, relatedness, compassion, issues relating to relationships and love.
Affirmation for the day	Key words: Forgiveness, Empathy, Compassion and Unconditional love "I am in touch with my need for revenge and transform it into compassion. I am in touch with my guilt and thus forgive myself. I am in touch with my expectations and transform them into unconditional love."

Day 10, 17 and 24

Throat Chakra

Chakra Name	Throat Chakra
Sanskrit Name, Meaning	Vishuddhi Chakra. Vishuddhi in Sanskrit means to purify. It has also been called the fountain of youth. It is the centre of expressive energy.
Location	Near the vocal chords
Color	Blue and Akash (Space/Ether) Element
Sense	Hearing
Endocrine System	Thyroid
Body System	Lymphatic
Physical Organs	Bronchial and vocal apparatus and digestive track
Emotions and Issues	Issues dealing with communication, creativity, and self expression.
Affirmation for the day	Key words: Self expression "I am in touch with my resistance to change and transform it into creative energy and powerful self expression."

Day 12, 19 and 26

Crown Chakra

Chakra Name	Crown Chakra
Sanskrit Name, Meaning	Sahasrara Chakra. Sahasrara literally means thousand-petal lotus. It is the centre of energies that are beyond human comprehension.
Location	Top of the skull
Affirmation for the day	"I am now at ease and ready to experience that which lies beyond. All is one and one is all. Reveal thy true nature, reveal thy glory."

THE SILVER LINING TECHNIQUE

Background:

This technique has been adapted from the ancient *Chakra Anusandhan Kriya*. It is an advanced technique of energizing the chakras. Commence this step of the 33 day chakra workout after completing the above 26 days of working with individual chakras. If for any reason you feel you are not ready go ahead and repeat another cycle of working with each chakra. The Silver Lining Technique forms the last seven days of this phase. To begin with, you could start off with 3 rotations and gradually increase it to a maximum of 9 rotations.

Note: As mentioned earlier, the seventh chakra Sahasrara or the thousand petal lotus is never described, as on the awakening of the sixth chakra or the third-eye chakra, it is said that the way to the final chakra is automatically revealed to the aspirant. Hence, on these days i.e. day 12, 19 and 26 you could spend ten to fifteen minutes silently contemplating and reflecting on all that has occurred over the past six days and allow the new experiences and information to assimilate.

Technique:

Step 1 Sit in a comfortable posture, with your spine erect.

Step2 Close your eyes and breathe normally.

Step3 Collect your awareness into your focused awareness point using the FVAT and allow it to rest in the root chakra, a few inches away.

Step 4 Allow your awareness to ascend slowly in front of your body, passing through all the chakras. You could mentally name them as you go along, but don't make a serious attempt to locate the chakras as you pass through them.

Step 5 Once your focused awareness point reaches the top of the head, i.e. the crown chakra, allow it to rest there for a few moments before allowing it to descend behind your body, again passing through all the chakras.

Step 6 Finally end up at the root chakra, thus completing one rotation. To facilitate the practice you could visualize a thin thread of silver light spinning all around you, slightly away from your body, surrounding you. The reason this technique is called the silver lining technique.

Phase III: Harmonization

The final phase of this program, is about getting hold of 'the' blissful state and allowing it to permeate through all the activities of the day, through all the areas of your life. By this time you have become aware of the issues that you are dealing with and the patterns that are now undesired. This is the most intensive phase, since you would be adding two very powerful exercises into the already existing routine from phase one. The Chakra workout is however unique to phase two. In other words you have basic practices with breathing and physical exercises, and you now add on the following exercises.

Note: Before you move to the next phase, make sure you have done a total of 36 rotations.

OM – The Sound of All Sounds

Background:

The sound of 'Om' has great significance in eastern spiritual practice. It is the combination of three basic sounds, namely, the 'a', 'u' and 'm'. It has been said to be the sound of all sounds. In Indian spirituality, chanting or listening to mantras are considered to be greatly relaxing and uplifting. It has been proved that meditating on the sound of 'Om' can have therapeutic effects on nerves, muscles, circulation and brain. The 'a' sound is produced when the mouth is completely open, the 'u' sound is made with the mouth half open and the 'm' sound with the lips sealed, thus covering the entire range of sounds that can be vocally produced. Since all worldly knowledge and understanding comes from words which are combinations of sounds, the Om is said to be the foundation of reality as we know it. It does not have any specific meaning or definition, but is said to represent *the all* and that which is beyond reality. The secret of this chanting practice is the fourth sound i.e. the silence between two chants. This is where you focus your awareness. You will find the effects of the vibrations thus produced as immediately and intensely relaxing.

Technique:

Step 1 Sit comfortably with your eyes closed. Begin with the 'breathe easy' exercise. Focus your awareness on the breath for about 5 minutes.

Step 2 Begin chanting 'Om' aloud with the out-breath and stretch it till your breath lasts, then in silence, take an in-breath. Give equal time to all three sounds; however, do stress the 'mmm' sound till it fades. Focus on the sounds for about 5 minutes.

Step 3 Continue chanting, but now only in your mind; in this step you don't chant aloud. Maintain your speed but change the chanting from the out- breath to the in-breath, now remaining silent with the out-breath. Visualize the sound getting internalized and focus on the internal sound for a few minutes.

Step 4 In this step, stop chanting completely. In the silence you would still be able to feel the vibrating pulse of the 'Om' sound resonating inside. Stay in this stillness for a few minutes and effortlessly absorb all the energy you have created. This energy will stay with you through the day, and within a few days of practice you will find it radiating to all those around you.

Manifesting New Realities

Background:

Creative visualization forms the basis for this technique. It is practiced in the morning and involves visualizing the major events of the day. This technique forms a 'dress rehearsal' for your main event which could be a meeting, a ceremony, an examination, or an interview, etc. Visualizing events proceeding smoothly and various aspects functioning properly, enables you to perform beyond your potential. In the actual event everything is familiar, hence, you will be comfortable and at complete ease. In addition, the technique helps clear out any interfering or negative images that might come in your way, and replace them with positive images. Olympic Gold medalist Mary Lou Retton, used visualization and imagery prior to all her splendid performances and recalls, *"I have always pictured myself positively. It gave me confidence. It was especially helpful in the Olympics, which were so important to me. I did all the routines in my head the night before the competition. Since I usually had trouble on the balance beam, I'd review that in my mind a lot, picturing myself landing straight on the beam."*

Some people have the ability to immediately visualize, whereas, for others it is a learned skill. If you belong to the second group, try this little activity to help improve your visualizing ability ~ wherever you are right now, look around and notice in-detail, the objects around you. Then close your eyes and try recreating the scene.

Technique:

Step 1 Sit comfortably with eyes closed. Begin taking nice-long-slow-deep breaths into your belly.

Step 2 Start by visualizing a pleasant scene, it could be the mountains, or the beach, a place that represents peace and quiet to you. Involve as many senses in this scenery as possible, hear, smell, taste, etc. Make it real for yourself.

Step 3 Say to yourself, "I am at peace" three times.

Step 4 Begin now to visualize the various events of your day, make sure you carry the relaxation and feeling of calm into all these events. Imagine everything moving well without any obstacles or hindrances. If you feel a certain person may have resistance to it you could mentally go up to him, pour your heart out and establish a new rapport. Go through the entire event right up to the desired outcome.

Step 5 After you have visualized all the major events of the day going well, visualize yourself returning home and spending quality time with your family and any other activity or interest. Finally visualize getting a good night's sleep.

Step 6 Declaring, "all is well", begin to slowly open your eyes and become aware of yourself and your environment.

References

1. "Stress Management for the Health of it" Clemson Extension, Cemson University, HE Leaflet 66, Rep. February 1997
2. "Complementory and Alternative Medicine Use Among Adults: United States 2002", Barnes P, Powell- Griner E, McFann K, Nahin R. CDC Advance Data Report 343, May 27, 2004
3. Excepted from "Relaxation therapy", Natural Standard, US and the Harvard Medical school faculty, Aetna IteliHealth, Harvard Medical Schools Consumer Health information website, updated Nov 10, 2003.
4. BBC News
5. "Relaxing music prevents stress induced anxiety, systolic blood pressure and heart rate in healthy males and females."- Knight WE, Richard PhD NS. Monash University, Victoria, Austrailia. J Music Ther. 2001 Winter, 38(4): 254-72

Disclaimer

'A Pocket Full of Peace' program and all its contents including the audio file and this program guide are for your personal and home use only. The guide book is for you to obtain the basic knowledge to support the recommended regimes. The information provided here is offered as a service and is not meant to replace any medical treatment. 'A Pocket Full of Peace' program cannot be construed as a recommendation of medication or treatment prescription for you to use suggested medications, herbs, or methods of therapy without supervision. It is not professed to be a physical or medical treatment nor is any such claim made. There are no medical recommendations or claims for 'A Pocket Full of Peace' program or for any of the regimens described in this book. All information provided here is only general health information and is only intended to facilitate communication between you and your healthcare provider/s. Readers are encouraged to confirm the information contained herein with other sources.

The information made available is not intended to be used as medical advice and is not intended to be used to diagnose, treat, cure or prevent any disease, nor should it be used for therapeutic purposes or as a substitute for your own health professional's advice. The program and its creators cannot guarantee, and assumes no legal liability or responsibility for the accuracy, currency or completeness of the information available through this book.

No individual should undertake the 'A Pocket Full of Peace' program or any of its regimens, practices and/or exercises without first consulting and obtaining the informed approval of a licensed medical practitioner. We make no warranties or representation as to the effectiveness of the 'A Pocket Full of Peace' program. No guarantee is made towards validity. Use the information at your own risk. In no event will Ray R Dharma, her staff, or anyone connected with this program be liable for damages of any kind arising from the use of this information including direct, indirect, consequential, incidental, special or punitive damages.

Any links to web sites in this booklet operated by third parties are provided for your convenience only. We are not responsible for the content and performance of these web sites or for your transactions with them. Mentioning of these web sites should not be taken to be an endorsement or a recommendation of any third party products or services offered by virtue of any information, material or content. As the user of links provided here, you are responsible for being aware of which organization is hosting the site they visit. It is your responsibility to make your own decisions about the accuracy, currency, reliability and correctness of the information contained in the mentioned web sites. You should be aware that the World Wide Web is an insecure public network that gives rise to the potential risk that a user's transactions are being viewed, intercepted or modified by third parties or that files which the user downloads may contain computer viruses or other defects. We accept no liability for any interference with or damage to your computer system, software or data. Users are encouraged to take appropriate and adequate precautions to ensure that whatever is selected from these sites is free of viruses or other contamination that may interfere with or damage your computer system, software or data.

You should carefully read all information provided by the manufacturers of the products on or in the product packaging and labels, before using any product recommended in this booklet.

'A Pocket Full of Peace' is a trademark for the rejuvenation and relaxation program designed by Ray R Dharma and all the content including the audio file and the regimes and exercises described in this book are subject to copyright. Any unauthorized duplication of any kind, public performance or broadcast is strictly prohibited and punishable as per laws applicable.

Recommended Reading

"Kundalini Yoga" by Swami Sivananda Radha, Motilal Banarasidas Publishers, 1992 or "Kundalini: Yoga for the West" by Swami Sivananda Radha, Timeless Books, 1978.

List of Recent Studies

Some of the more recent studies are listed below:

Arntz A. Cognitive therapy versus applied relaxation as treatment of generalized anxiety disorder. Behav Res Ther 2003;Jun, 41(6): 633-646.

Beck JG, Stanley MA, Baldwin LE, et al. Comparison of cognitive therapy and relaxation training for panic disorder. J Consult Clin Psychol 1994;62(4):818-826.

Berger AM, VonEssen S, Kuhn BR, et al. Adherence, sleep, and fatigue outcomes after adjuvant breast cancer chemotherapy: results of a feasibility intervention study. Oncol Nurs Forum 2003;May-Jun, 30(3):513-522.

Biggs QM, Kelly KS, Toney JD. The effects of deep diaphragmatic breathing and focused attention on dental anxiety in a private practice setting. J Dent Hyg 2003;Spring, 77(2):105-113.

Blanchard EB, Appelbaum KA, Guarnieri P, et al. Five year prospective follow-up on the treatment of chronic headache with biofeedback and/or relaxation. Headache 1987;27(10):580-583.

Borkovec TD, Newman MG, Pincus AL, Lytle R. A component analysis of cognitive-behavioral therapy for generalized anxiety disorder and the role of interpersonal problems. J Consult Clin Psychol 2002;Apr, 70(2):288-298.

Broota A, Dhir R. Efficacy of two relaxation techniques in depression. J Pers Clin Stud 1990;6:83-90.

Carroll D, Seers K. Relaxation for the relief of chronic pain: a systematic review. J Adv Nurs 1998;27(3):476-487.

Cheung YL, Molassiotis A, Chang AM. The effect of progressive muscle relaxation training on anxiety and quality of life after stoma surgery in colorectal cancer patients. Psychooncology 2003;Apr-May, 12(3):254-266.

Cimprich B, Ronis DL. An environmental intervention to restore attention in women with newly diagnosed breast cancer. Cancer Nurs 2003;Aug, 26(4):284-292. Quiz, 293-294.

Deckro GR, Ballinger KM, Hoyt M, et al. The evaluation of a mind/body intervention to reduce psychological distress and perceived stress in college students. J Am Coll Health 2002;May, 50(6):281-287.

Delaney JP, Leong KS, Watkins A, Brodie D. The short-term effects of myofascial trigger point massage therapy on cardiac autonomic tone in healthy subjects. J Adv Nurs 2002;Feb, 37(4):364-371.

Diette GB, Lechtzin N, Haponik E, et al. Distraction therapy with nature sights and sounds reduces pain during flexible bronchoscopy: a complementary approach to routine analgesia. Chest 2003;Mar, 123(3):941-948.

Edelen C, Perlow M. A comparison of the effectiveness of an opioid analgesic and a nonpharmacologic intervention to improve incentive spirometry volumes. Pain Manag Nurs 2002;Mar, 3(1):36-42.

Egner T, Strawson E, Gruzelier JH. EEG signature and phenomenology of alpha/theta neurofeedback training versus mock feedback. Appl Psychophysiol Biofeedback 2002;Dec, 27(4):261-270.

Engel JM, Rapoff MA, Pressman AR. Long-term follow-up of relaxation training for pediatric headache disorders. Headache 1992;32(3):152-156.

Eppley KR, Abrams AI, Shear J. Differential effects of relaxation techniques on trait anxiety: a meta-analysis. J Clin Psychol 1989;45(6):957-974.

Fors EA, Sexton H, Gotestam KG. The effect of guided imagery and amitriptyline on daily fibromyalgia pain: a prospective, randomized, controlled trial. J Psychiatr Res 2002;May-Jun, 36(3):179-187.

Foster RL, Yucha CB, Zuk J, Vojir CP. Physiologic correlates of comfort in healthy children. Pain Manag Nurs 2003;Mar, 4(1):23-30.

Gay MC, Philippot P, Luminet O. Differential effectiveness of psychological interventions for reducing osteoarthritis pain: a comparison of Erikson [correction of Erickson] hypnosis and Jacobson relaxation. Eur J Pain 2002;6(1):1-16.

Ginsburg GS, Drake KL. School-based treatment for anxious african-american adolescents: a controlled pilot study. J Am Acad Child Adolesc Psychiatry 2002;Jul, 41(7):768-775.

Good M, Anderson GC, Stanton-Hicks M, et al. Relaxation and music reduce pain after gynecologic surgery. Pain Manag Nurs 2002;Jun, 3(2):61-70.

Good M, Stanton-Hicks M, Grass JA, et al. Relaxation and music to reduce postsurgical pain. J Adv Nurs 2001;33(2):208-215.

Goodale IL, Domar AD, Benson H. Alleviation of premenstrual syndrome symptoms with the relaxation response. Obstet Gynecol 1990;75(4):649-655.

Greist JH, Marks IM, Baer L, et al. Behavior therapy for obsessive-compulsive disorder guided by a computer or by a clinician compared with relaxation as a control. J Clin Psychiatry 2002;Feb, 63(2):138-145.

Grover N, Kumaraiah V, Prasadrao PS, D'Souza G. Cognitive behavioural intervention in bronchial asthma. J Assoc Physicians India 2002;Jul, 50:896-900.

Halpin LS, Speir AM, CapoBianco P, Barnett SD. Guided imagery in cardiac surgery. Outcomes Manag 2002;Jul-Sep, 6(3):132-137.

Hanley J, Stirling P, Brown C. Randomised controlled trial of therapeutic massage in the management of stress. Br J Gen Pract 2003;Jan, 53(486):20-25.

Harvey L, Inglis SJ, Espie CA. Insomniacs' reported use of CBT components and relationship to long-term clinical outcome. Behav Res Ther 2002;Jan, 40(1):75-83.

Hattan J, King L, Griffiths P. The impact of foot massage and guided relaxation following cardiac surgery: a randomized controlled trial. J Adv Nurs 2002;Jan, 37(2):199-207.

Hockemeyer J, Smyth J. Evaluating the feasibility and efficacy of a self-administered manual-based stress management intervention for individuals with asthma: results from a controlled study. Behav Med 2002;Winter, 27(4):161-172.

Houghton LA, Calvert EL, Jackson NA, et al. Visceral sensation and emotion: a study using hypnosis. Gut 2002;Nov, 51(5):701-704.

Irvin JH, Domar AD, Clark C, et al. The effects of relaxation response training on menopausal symptoms. J Psychosom Obstet Gynaecol 1996;17(4):202-207.

Jacob RG, Chesney MA, Williams DM, et al. Relaxation therapy for hypertension: design effects and treatment effects. Ann Behav Med 1991;13(1):5-17.

Jacobs GD, Rosenberg PA, Friedman R, et al. Multifactor behavioral treatment of chronic sleep-onset insomnia using stimulus control and the relaxation response: a preliminary study. Behav Modif 1993;17(4):498-509.

Kircher T, Teutsch E, Wormstall H, et al. Effects of autogenic training in elderly patients [Article in German]. Z Gerontol Geriatr 2002;Apr, 35(2):157-165.

Kober A, Scheck T, Schubert B, et al. Auricular acupressure as a treatment for anxiety in prehospital transport settings. Anesthesiology 2003;Jun, 98(6):1328-1332.

Kohen DP. Relaxation/mental imagery (self-hypnosis) for childhood asthma: behavioral outcomes in a prospective, controlled study. Hypnos 1995;22:132-144.

Kroener-Herwig B, Denecke H. Cognitive-behavioral therapy of pediatric headache: are there differences in efficacy between a therapist-administered group training and a self-help format? J Psychosom Res 2002;Dec, 53(6):1107-1114.

Kroner-Herwig B, Frenzel A, Fritsche G, et al. The management of chronic tinnitus: comparison of an outpatient cognitive-behavioral group training to minimal-contact interventions. J Psychosom Res 2003;Apr, 54(4):381-389.

Lechner SC, Antoni MH, Lydston D, et al. Cognitive-behavioral interventions improve quality of life in women with AIDS. J Psychosom Res 2003;Mar, 54(3):253-261.

Lee DW, Chan KW, Poon CM, et al. Relaxation music decreases the dose of patient-controlled sedation during colonoscopy: a prospective randomized controlled trial. Gastrointest Endosc 2002;Jan, 55(1):33-36.

Lemstra M, Stewart B, Olszynski WP. Effectiveness of multidisciplinary intervention in the treatment of migraine: a randomized clinical trial. Headache 2002;Oct, 42(9):845-854.

Leng TR, Woodward MJ, Stokes MJ, et al. Effects of multisensory stimulation in people with Huntington's disease: a randomized controlled pilot study. Clin Rehabil 2003;Feb, 17(1):30-41.

Lewin RJ, Furze G, Robinson J, et al. A randomised controlled trial of a self-management plan for patients with newly diagnosed angina. Br J Gen Pract 2002;Mar, 52(476):194-196, 199-201.

Lewin RJ, Thompson DR, Elton RA. Trial of the effects of an advice and relaxation tape given within the first 24 h of admission to hospital with acute myocardial infarction. Int J Cardiol 2002;Feb, 82(2):107-114. Discussion, 115-116.

Lichstein KL, Peterson BA, Riedel BW, et al. Relaxation to assist sleep medication withdrawal. Behav Modif 1999;23(3):379-402.

Livanou M, Basoglu M, Marks IM, et al. Beliefs, sense of control and treatment outcome in post-traumatic stress disorder. Psychol Med 2002;Jan, 32(1):157-165.

Machiko T, Katsutaro N, Chika O. A study of psychoneuroendocrinological effects of music therapy [Article in Japanese]. Seishin Shinkeigaku Zasshi 2003;105(4):468-472.

Mandle CL, Jacobs SC, Arcari PM, et al. The efficacy of relaxation response interventions with adult patients: a review of the literature. J Cardiovasc Nurs 1996;10(3):4-26.

Mastenbroek I, McGovern L. The effectiveness of relaxation techniques in controlling chemotherapy induced nausea: a literature review. Austral Occupat Ther J 1991;38(3):137-142.

Mataix-Cols D, Marks IM, Greist JH, et al. Obsessive-compulsive symptom dimensions as predictors of compliance with and response to behaviour therapy: results from a controlled trial. Psychother Psychosom 2002;Sep-Oct, 71(5):255-262.

McCain NL, Munjas BA, Munro CL, et al. Effects of stress management on PNI-based outcomes in persons with HIV disease. Res Nurs Health 2003;Apr, 26(2):102-117.

Morley S, Eccleston C, Williams A. Systematic review and meta-analysis of randomized controlled trials of cognitive behaviour therapy and behaviour therapy for chronic pain in adults, excluding headache. Pain 1999;80(1-2):1-13.

NIH Technology Assessment Panel on Integration of Behavioral and Relaxation Approaches into the Treatment of Chronic Pain and Insomnia. Integration of behavioral and relaxation approaches into the treatment of chronic pain and insomnia. JAMA 1996;276(4):313-318.

Okvat HA, Oz MC, Ting W, Namerow PB. Massage therapy for patients undergoing cardiac catheterization. Altern Ther Health Med 2002;May-Jun, 8(3):68-70, 72, 74-75.

Ost LG, Breitholtz E. Applied relaxation vs. cognitive therapy in the treatment of generalized anxiety disorder. Behav Res Ther 2000;38(8):777-790.

Pallesen S, Nordhus IH, Kvale G, et al. Behavioral treatment of insomnia in older adults: an open clinical trial comparing two interventions. Behav Res Ther 2003;Jan, 41(1):31-48.

Passchier J, van den Bree MB, Emmen HH, et al. Relaxation training in school classes does not reduce headache complaints. Headache 1990;30(10):660-664.

Pawlow LA, O'Neil PM, Malcolm RJ. Night eating syndrome: effects of brief relaxation training on stress, mood, hunger, and eating patterns. Int J Obes Relat Metab Disord 2003;Aug, 27(8):970-978.

Petersen RW, Quinlivan JA. Preventing anxiety and depression in gynaecological cancer: a randomised controlled trial. BJOG 2002;Apr, 109(4):386-394.

Piazza-Waggoner CA, Cohen LL, Kohli K, Taylor BK. Stress management for dental students performing their first pediatric restorative procedure. J Dent Educ 2003;May, 67(5):542-548.

Popova EI, Ivonin AA, Shuvaev VT, Mikheev VF. Neurophysiological mechanisms of acquisition of fear-resistance habit controlled by biological feedback displayed by skin galvanic response [Article in Russian]. Zh Vyssh Nerv Deiat Im I P Pavlova 2002;Sep-Oct, 52(5):563-569.

Rankin EJ, Gilner FH, Gfeller JD, et al. Efficacy of progressive muscle relaxation for reducing state anxiety among elderly adults on memory tasks. Percept Mot Skills 1993;77(3 Pt 2):1395-1402.

Renzi C, Peticca L, Pescatori M. The use of relaxation techniques in the perioperative management of proctological patients: preliminary results. Int J Colorectal Dis 2000;15(5-6):313-316.

Richards SC, Scott DL. Prescribed exercise in people with fibromyalgia: parallel group randomised controlled trial. BMJ 2002;Jul 27, 325(7357):185.

Rybarczyk B, Lopez M, Benson R, et al. Efficacy of two behavioral treatment programs for comorbid geriatric insomnia. Psychol Aging 2002;Jun, 17(2):288-298.

Sander Wint S, Eshelman D, Steele J, Guzzetta CE. Effects of distraction using virtual reality glasses during lumbar punctures in adolescents with cancer. Oncol Nurs Forum 2002;Jan-Feb, 29(1):E8-E15.

Schofield P. Evaluating Snoezelen for relaxation within chronic pain management. Br J Nurs 2002;Jun 27-Jul 10, 11(12):812-821.

Schofield P, Payne S. A pilot study into the use of a multisensory environment (Snoezelen) within a palliative day-care setting. Int J Palliat Nurs 2003;Mar, 9(3):124-130. Erratum in: Int J Palliat Nurs 2003;Apr, 9(4):178.

Seers K, Carroll D. Relaxation techniques for acute pain management: a systematic review. J Adv Nurs 1998;27(3):466-475.

Shapiro SL, Bootzin RR, Figueredo AJ, et al. The efficacy of mindfulness-based stress reduction in the treatment of sleep disturbance in women with breast cancer: an exploratory study. J Psychosom Res 2003;Jan, 54(1):85-91.

Sheu S, Irvin BL, Lin HS, Mar CL. Effects of progressive muscle relaxation on blood pressure and psychosocial status for clients with essential hypertension in Taiwan. Holist Nurs Pract 2003;Jan-Feb, 17(1):41-47.

Sloman R. Relaxation and imagery for anxiety and depression control in community patients with advanced cancer. Cancer Nurs 2002;Dec, 25(6):432-435.

Smith DW, Arnstein P, Rosa KC, Wells-Federman C. Effects of integrating therapeutic touch into a cognitive behavioral pain treatment program: report of a pilot clinical trial. J Holist Nurs 2002;Dec, 20(4):367-387.

Smith PM, Reilly KR, Houston Miller N, et al. Application of a nurse-managed inpatient smoking cessation program. Nicotine Tob Res 2002;May, 4(2):211-222.

Smolen D, Topp R, Singer L. The effect of self-selected music during colonoscopy on anxiety, heart rate, and blood pressure. Appl Nurs Res 2002;Aug, 15(3):126-136.

Stallibrass C, Sissons P, Chalmers C. Randomized controlled trial of the Alexander technique for idiopathic Parkinson's disease. Clin Rehabil 2002;Nov, 16(7):695-708.

Targ EF, Levine EG. The efficacy of a mind-body-spirit group for women with breast cancer: a randomized controlled trial. Gen Hosp Psychiatry 2002;Jul-Aug, 24(4):238-248.

Turner-Stokes L, Erkeller-Yuksel F, Miles A, et al. Outpatient cognitive behavioral pain management programs: a randomized comparison of a group-based multidisciplinary versus an individual therapy model. Arch Phys Med Rehabil 2003;Jun, 84(6):781-788.

Tyni-Lenne R, Stryjan S, Eriksson B, et al. Beneficial therapeutic effects of physical training and relaxation therapy in women with coronary syndrome X. Physiother Res Int 2002;7(1):35-43.

Van Dixhoorn JJ, Duivenvoorden HJ. Effect of relaxation therapy on cardiac events after myocardial infarction: a 5-year follow-up study. J Cardiopulm Rehabil 1999;19(3):178-185.

Viens M, De Koninck J, Mercier P, et al. Trait anxiety and sleep-onset insomnia: evaluation of treatment using anxiety management training. J Psychosom Res 2003;Jan, 54(1):31-37.

Viljanen M, Malmivaara A, Uitti J, et al. Effectiveness of dynamic muscle training, relaxation training, or ordinary activity for chronic neck pain: randomised controlled trial. BMJ 2003;Aug 30, 327(7413):475.

Walker LG, Walker MB, Ogston K, et al. Psychological, clinical and pathological effects of relaxation training and guided imagery during primary chemotherapy. Br J Cancer 1999;80(1-2):262-268.

Wang H, Jiang S, Yang W, Han D. Tinnitus retraining therapy: a clinical control study of 117 patients [Article in Chinese]. Zhonghua Yi Xue Za Zhi 2002;Nov 10, 82(21):1464-1467.

Wang SM, Caldwell-Andrews AA, Kain ZN. The use of complementary and alternative medicines by surgical patients: a follow-up survey study. Anesth Analg 2003;Oct, 97(4):1010-1015.

Wilhelm S, Deckersbach T, Coffey BJ, et al. Habit reversal versus supportive psychotherapy for Tourette's disorder: a randomized controlled trial. Am J Psychiatry 2003;Jun, 160(6):1175-1177.

Willumsen T, Vassend O. Effects of cognitive therapy, applied relaxation and nitrous oxide sedation: a five-year follow-up study of patients treated for dental fear. Acta Odontol Scand 2003;Apr, 61(2):93-99.

Wynd CA. Relaxation imagery used for stress reduction in the prevention of smoking relapse. J Adv Nurs 1992;17(3):294-302.

Credits

Research by Unalome Project - By Shaurya Singh

Author's Photograph - By Siddharth Shah

Illustrations - By Apurva S Kapoor

About the Author

For more than 30 years, Ray R Dharma's passion has been helping people EMPOWER and take their lives to another level, in the areas that matter most: intimate relationships, careers and health.

She was initiated into the Reiki practice - a formal modality of Cosmic healing, in the year 1993 and the Sensei levels in 1995-96. The name 'Ray R Dharma' was blessed upon her by a Tibetan Buddhist Monk in the year 1997, with the initiation into the Tibetan Buddhist Mantra of the White Tara, the patron Saint of Compassion, Women and Children. Her initiation into Transcendental Meditation in 2000 marked the beginning of an intense inward journey. She dedicated herself in accelerating the awakening of the Inner Strength and consciousness, with the practice of Shivyog and Sri Vidya Sadhana.

Her personal practices have helped her profoundly enhance her sensitivity, serenity, kinesthetic ability, creativity and resilience. Ray's teachings in your life act as a guide to living a life of greater purpose and sacred presence. Her seminar trainings and audios have guided and empowered people from all walks of life.

(Attached here with are some of my press interviews:)

1. https://drive.google.com/file/d/1dnHVKuMKPXCUSbzwIocXlUCH GZ9CUf_M/view?usp=sharing

2. https://timesofindia.indiatimes.com/life-style/spotlight/these-bengalureans-vouch-for-the-power-of-gratitude/articleshow/88145744.cms